A Lifelong Journey - The Road to a Biblical Worldview

Mark Anthony

Published by Mark Anthony, 2024.

While every precaution has been taken in the preparation of this book, the publisher assumes no responsibility for errors or omissions, or for damages resulting from the use of the information contained herein.

A LIFELONG JOURNEY - THE ROAD TO A BIBLICAL WORLDVIEW

First edition. January 8, 2024.

ISBN: 979-8224823512

Written by Mark Anthony.

Table of Contents

Special recognition and sincere appreciation belongs solely to my wife Rebecca of 37 years, without whose sincere patience and love, this work would have never been brought to a completion.

Introduction / Prelude

Growing up as a young boy and into my teenage years, my family would move from place to place fairly often on what seemed to be an annual basis. We lived mainly in middle America from Montana to Louisiana, having family roots that originated in Oklahoma and as I reached my young adult years I settled down in Missouri. From what I recall of my early years, my mom had divorced before I could even remember. She had a Baptist background but I do not recall attending church before turning 6 years old. She married my stepdad when I was about 6 years old and he had a strong Methodist background. In fact, I recall my Methodist water baptism when we became church members. On a regular basis, my mom and stepdad made it a duty to attend church most Sunday's, attend Sunday school regularly, participate in church potluck dinners and attend other various fellowship gatherings. Later in life, I discovered that my biological dad also had a Baptist background, but he had prided himself by living in a humanistic unbelieving lifestyle for most of his life. He had also claimed the catholic church was the only authority. While living and growing up with my mom and stepdad, we were sort of proud of the fact our home had a huge King James family bible that occupied a prominent location on top of our living room coffee table. This Bible was ornately decorated and had a picture of Jesus on the front cover. It appeared to be about 6 inches thick. One might ask if this Bible made any difference during this time in our lives? Looking back, in all honesty - not really. We applied some biblical principles that we learned in the churches we attended, but not necessarily in the right way of living them. On the other hand, we thought of ourselves as good descent American Christian people.

As I think back to those early years in my life, I could sense there seemed to be something missing. We were not able to identify what that was, because in another sense, we also thought we were a normal

American family. This meant to us that we were okay, acceptable normal middle-class folks. Honestly, our lives were centered around having friends, watching tv shows and attending movies at the theaters. I recall we would make a point to watch a few holiday movies and television, such as - The Ten Commandments, It's a Wonderful Life, Spartacus, and Ben Hur, on an annual basis. For all we knew they were stories that were related to God and Jesus. Attending church was important, but it wasn't necessarily at the top of our list of things we looked forward to doing each week.

Please understand, this brief testimony is in no way intended to disparage denominational churches like the Methodist church we attended, nor any other non-denominational church we visited. As a young teenager, it was through a Methodist lay-witness mission event at our church where Jesus was introduced to us in a way that we hadn't ever heard before. In short, this event could have been described as a mini revival. Shortly thereafter, some in our church desired more of the spiritual things of God and others desired to go back to the style of church that they had before the missionary event. Unfortunately, this church split, and our family ended up being excommunicated from their local membership and the Methodist church. Although there are times of trouble like this that do occur from time to time in the body of Christ, God does not and will not forget the denominational churches that continue to follow Him. The movement of the Holy Spirit continues to this day within these churches of America and those around the world.

Growing up as a teenager in the 1970's, the charismatic renewal movement was becoming well known among our circle of friends in our community. This movement had a profound effect and change on my immediate family. As my family increased our involvement in the local church, I'd have to say there were many things in this life we lived that presented many conflicts of thought and reason that were begging the questions within my heart and mind of "what, who, why and how?"

My head knowledge and heart knowledge became divided and there was a great conflict within me.

After the excommunication, our friends and my family began attending local Pentecostal churches and other various type meetings where there were certain moving's and prophetic declarations from Holy Spirit that appeared strange and unusual at this time. I had many teenage friends who were involved with Baptist churches and other denominations. Even as I participated in church and in the charismatic movement, I still had a restless heart and mind in the things of God along with the conflicting thoughts from this world system. Scripture describes this kind of person as being a double-minded man, and unstable in all his ways. That scripture in the book of James perfectly described my identity.

It's unfortunate, that our local churches at that time did not appear to us to be equipped to provide many answers, or responses, nor insight into many of the questions in this life with regard to "what, who, why and how." By all appearance, churches had their doctrines which appeared contrary to what was taught in local schools, given their own evolutionary theories on life and their own brand of truth. Admittedly, if there's any further honesty and vulnerability on my part to be added into this, as an American teenager and young adult, there was also the issue of emotions with raging hormones and not knowing or understanding anything in regard to self-control in the lusts of my flesh and the lust for this world.

There were then as there are now, many conflicts in the home and at the school, among parents and teachers, between parents, teachers and local school boards. And over the most recent couple of generations in our society, these conflicts and problems have progressively been getting worse. Growing up and being educated in the public-school system of the 1960's and 1970's, this was difficult from the simple aspect of not knowing who was really telling or teaching us the truth. I grew up with the conflict of natural-minded man proclaiming they know the truth of natural history and where man came from, whereas the church was proclaiming a different kind of truth based solely on what appeared to be a blind faith in spiritual things without much physical evidence available.

Please realize, I'm expressing the thoughts of an ignorant young man during that time. I grew up during the time of local pastors teaching a lot of dos and don'ts (law) regarding things related to our flesh. I don't remember having an understanding of faith and how any of the spiritual things in the Bible related to our physical lives, nor how God interacted with His people on a personal level. His word wasn't alive to me, and He always seemed to be distant, way out there in space and uninterested. Now that I'm 63 years young at the time of this writing, I've since learned this is not true and I'm able to say that God is very interested in all of us, and He is closer to us than we may think He is.

As you read this narrative, you may begin to recognize that eventually the questions in the heart and mind of that young boy, teenager and adult have now been answered. And, that much later in life a perspective has been developed that provides steady guidance in my life today and in Christ. Some would refer to this as having a Biblical worldview. It's my hope this narrative may be a help to you on your journey through your life to a much deeper relationship with God.

We will start with the beginning of the Bible, the book of Genesis. And in doing so, there will be biblical references and perceptions introduced that will be contributing to an overall scripturally based perspective. It is vitally important for believers in Christ to become more familiar with our spiritual history. Much of what will be presented in the following chapters will be new, even for many Christians. One example is that many Christians do not realize that though the Bible starts at the beginning with creation, there are things presented later in the Bible that relate to the front of the book and things in the front of the book that relate to things in the back of the book.

The focus will be to help believers develop in their knowledge of Christ and in personal relationship with God our Father and grow in their love of Christ. It doesn't matter if you're a brand-new believer, or whether you've been a believer for many years. Even, if you're completely unfamiliar with the scriptures, or spiritual things, please don't quit and give into the pressures around you. Give this process time and allow Holy Spirit to reveal the Bible to you on a personal level. Truly, this narrative is only intended as a help or a guide. Although, I will give a preliminary warning here, there might be a few things mentioned which may in some way appear to conflict with some doctrines or other denominational church doctrine. It is not my intent to replace what you may choose to believe or your church doctrine. And it is not intended to replace your Bible. If anything, it is only intended to encourage believers to pursue Him more boldly in their life because He chose to love us first before we even knew who He was. In fact, John 17, Jesus reveals that the Father loves us just as much as He loves His son Jesus. Given this revelation, I was inspired to start drafting this book in 2022 shortly after reading a Christian news article regarding the present-day issue of the severe lack of many Christians, roughly 10% that actually have a Biblical worldview. Reading this article sort of broke my heart for my fellow brothers and sisters in the Lord. We live in times of unprecedented levels of unbelief in our society today.

In reading this, if you find areas of disagreement, that's ok. It won't be taken personally. None of us are perfect in knowledge nor have all knowledge, and I'm not one to make such a prideful claim. The only thing I might claim is, this life on earth is a journey. Our entire life here is testing ground of our faith and our eventual eternal future with Him.

All Christian believers are on many diverse levels of intellectual and spiritual understanding as well as different levels of faith, thus we are referred to as disciples. Allow me to further explain that I'm only a man, and I am very capable of missing the mark. On the other hand, I've lived a few years and there are some things that I've learned and experienced over the years in my life in Christ. I've learned to recognize that God's Word takes precedence over any opinion, and narrative, including all of the circumstances and experiences that occur in life.

This narrative will not go into the details of my life. The reason is, there were many ignorant and stupid things I allowed in my life. Many things in my past are disappointing and truly not even worth dwelling on. What I can reveal is that in 2010, when I was 50 years young, I rededicated my life to the Lord after some serious issues had occurred in the life of my family. Personally, I was on the brink of self-destruction. Yet, I had sense enough to ask the Lord for revelation, understanding and for answers in the issues of my life. For personal reasons, I didn't want the regular religious answers that are in the foundations of the various doctrines of Christian faith that so many tend to rely on. Those doctrinal answers weren't going to work for me. And, I didn't have much tolerance for the psychological and psychiatric reasonings of man. What I desired was scriptural evidence and insight by the Holy Spirit. Once I chose to submit to the Lord completely, He guided me to the many answers needed for my life-long questions. Answers that were in His word the entire time, if only I had looked for them when I was younger, I'm sure my life and choices may have been different.

The Apostle Paul provides a wonderful example of attitude in life, that is, to lay aside those things which are behind and pursue the prize of the upward call of Christ, setting his mind on things above, not on the things that are here on earth. (Philippians 3: 13 & Colossians 3: 2) He was well aware of what he did before meeting Christ on the road to Damascus, but he lived his new life in Christ forgiven and with unqualified commitment to the One who saved him. So will I, because in his writings he instructed us to imitate him as he imitated Christ in his life. (1Corinthians 11:1) This doesn't mean I will suddenly forget those things behind me in the past, but it's a choice to leave them behind and move forward into a deeper, fulfilling, faithful and obedient lifestyle in Christ. And it doesn't mean I think that I've arrived at perfection, nor that I won't have opportunity to sin in the future. But for those who are saved, we are all called to grow to a place of spiritual maturity in Christ.

A well-known missionary and healing minister from the early 1900's named John G. Lake once said the following," The real Christian is a separated man. He is separated forever unto God in all the departments of his life. So his body and his soul and his spirit are forever committed to his Father above... A hundred-fold consecration takes the individual forever out of the hands of all, but God."

Liardon, "John G. Lake," 328.

Chapter 1 – What am I? (Where did I come from?)

The formative years as a teenager and into my young adult years, these were the most difficult years in reconciling belief in a God above with what was considered the belief system in this world and what was happening daily. I was existing on what the Bible describes as carnal natural-minded living. There is a scripture in Ephesians 4:17-19 which perfectly describes my early life as follows:

> "...you should no longer walk as the rest of the Gentiles walk, in the futility of their mind, having their understanding darkened, being alienated from the life of God, because of the ignorance that is in them, because of the blindness of their heart, who being past feeling, have given themselves over to lewdness, to work all uncleanness with greediness." (NKJV)

The word Gentile simply means one who doesn't know God. Though I had been saved at an early age through the work of the lay-witness mission, there was no real spiritual direction available during these formative years. Baby-boomer Americans will understand when I write that our generation was not necessarily raised by parents who knew better. Like many of us, I was raised to think and believe selfishly by parents, our local godless school education, the constant peer-pressure of school friends and by our evening ritual devotion to watching godless television programs. When I left home as a young adult to head out into this world, I wasn't prepared for what was ahead of me in life. I was living and existing like a Gentile unbeliever as the scripture said. Ultimately, there came a point to where I was having to make a choice. Whether I was going to believe in God above, or to not believe. In my heart I knew the scripture "to seek first the kingdom of God and His righteousness..." But I honestly didn't know what righteousness meant for me, nor how to apply this verse in my life. (Righteousness simply means right standing with God, right living in His ways.) The good news is that I eventually made the right choice to believe. It is in the following paragraphs that sets a foundation and begins a path of understanding toward having a Biblical worldview.

While reading through the first three chapters of the book of Genesis, the creation is described in detail of the heavens, the universe, the stars, the galaxies, the sun and planets, then this earth, with all living things, and the creatures on the earth. Then, God finishes all of this in creating a man. God breathed His breath of life into the first man, Adam. He becomes the first-born of God, created in the image and likeness of God. A short time after, Eve is created from the side of Adam, not as the lesser of the two, but as an equal with him. This beginning of the book is important, we should not treat this as a minor thing. Medical science has revealed how we are intricately designed creatures.

Let us ponder a moment. If we were able to watch Adam, as he stood and walked next to God side by side in the Garden of Eden, they would appear and look exactly alike, mirror images of each other. Adam was created with godly character, attitudes, integrity, personality, wisdom, understanding, knowledge, intelligence, including the attributes of God's goodness, joy, peace, patience, kindness, gentleness, self-control, faith, hope and love. From the New Testament (Galatians 5:22) we understand these to be fruits of the Spirit. The same attributes of God were breathed into and were intended to be at the very core of Adam's life and being. Unfortunately, there are many people who actually believe Adam was somehow created to be a weak, vulnerable and flawed human being leading them to think that Adam's failure was all part of God's plan and sovereign will. Nothing could be further from the truth. This is called human reasoning and does not align with the creation that was made perfect and was good in the eyes of God. We can read for ourselves that in the beginning, everything God created was initially perfect and had no flaws, nor any curse in this earth.

The noticeable difference between God and Adam was that the physical body of Adam was made from the dust or dirt of this earth. A flesh, blood and bone body was created and formed for the spirit and soul of man to live in. God designed this body to physically exist on this planet. The other creatures on earth also have similar bodies, but they were not given a living soul as the man. Given this, the Bible reveals that God is spirit (John 4:24). God created man to have his own spirit with a living soul to live in a body and occupy this world. There are some who speculate that Adam was also created having the light of God's glory surrounding him which covered his body before his fall from grace into sin. Their speculation is partially based on how Adam and Eve reacted after their act of sin in an attempt to cover themselves with fig leaf's, by noticing their nakedness after their sin took place. Recall the transfiguration of Jesus referenced in Matthew 17:2. This is when Jesus became radiantly white as the light and His face shined like the sun when He was up on the mountain with Peter, James and John. The speculation makes sense, but Adam's appearance before his sin cannot be scripturally proven but makes for an interesting discussion because the New Testament also refers to Jesus as the second Adam. It is a wonder that before sin, Adam and Eve were able to stand in the presence and glory of God and fellowship freely with one another. Later in the Old Testament, we find that after the sin of Adam that a person would die if they were physically able to look upon the face of God.

As noted above, there are some who assume that Adam and Eve were created with an innocence and understanding of a child, and lacked knowing anything, thus giving an excuse for human reasoning as to why they might have fallen into sin, thereby reasoning it was God's will. This justifies their doctrinal position for supposing that since people and believers sin all the time and are unable to get away from it, we might as well continue living this life in sin. Personally, and Biblically, I do not agree with this human reasoning and its contrary to what the Bible reveals. Adam had to be highly intelligent, because he was created to be "like God, in His image." In Genesis, we read where Adam names all the animals, the cattle, the birds of the air and beast of the field. Naming all these creatures takes intelligence. I'd be curious to know if he took the time to give a name to the creeping things on the earth, a half a million different species of bugs. One day in heaven, I'll get to ask Adam that question.

Remember, in the New Testament, Jesus challenged the religious rulers of His day; He quoted from the book of Psalms, recognizing that all of mankind are gods on the earth (Psalms 82:6; John 10:34). While the animals were being presented for Adam to give them names, he noticed that he was alone, because the animals that were presented to him were male and female. God knew it was not good for Adam to be alone. God had a pleasant surprise for him, He made Eve. Adam obviously loved what he saw, and he received her as a valuable and honorable gift from God. Adam said she is "bone of my bone and flesh of my flesh." One man and one woman, together they are viewed by God as one flesh in this union. God institutes this marriage, this union, to be between a man and a woman. Jesus clearly communicated this truth in the New Testament in His lecture with the religious rulers found in Mark 10:5-9. God didn't make a mistake with the marriage union of male with female.

God has not ever made a mistake. Since the fall of Adam, what we're witnessing in society today is nothing new. From ancient millennia non-believing mankind has been under constant satanic influence and this contributes to the distortions and deceptions of human psychological thinking and various kinds of political reasonings giving them a godless direction in a self-destructive life on this earth. Today we have a godless amoral society, confused in thought, emotion and in their identity as either a man or as a woman, even though they have the physical parts on their bodies to prove what and who they are in creation. And, as a result of their pride, that is, their choice to be stubborn in their own reasoning and emotions, their unwillingness to admit what they do is abnormal and is a perversion of their creation, they've chosen to justify themselves in their own minds. (Romans 1: 18-30)

Presently, there is no man that can fully describe all of who God is. We gather from scripture He is all knowing, present in all places at all times, all powerful and is always good. God is a three-part being and in Genesis 1:26 He states, "Let us make man in Our image, according to Our likeness..."(NKJV) In the Old Testament, God had to reveal Himself and His character to His people through His Name. He is known by many names; the following are thirty-three (33) Hebrew Names given in scripture. For the sake of limited time, I'll list the names and allow you to study their full meaning for yourself.

EL - God

ELOHIM – God, Creator

ELOHIM CHAYIM – The Living God

El SHADDAI – God Almighty or God All-Sufficient

ADONAI – Master or Lord

YAHWEH or JEHOVAH – Lord or Self-Existent One

YAHWEH-JIREH – Lord will Provide

YAHWEH-ROPHE – Lord who Heals

YAHWEH-NISSI – Lord our Banner

YAHWEH-M'KADDESH – Lord who Sanctifies

YAHWEH-SHALOM - Lord our Peace

YAHWEH-ELOHIM – Lord God

YAHWEH-TSIDKENU – Lord our Righteousness

YAHWEH-ROHI – Lord our Shepherd

YAHWEH-SHAMMAH – Lord is There

YAHWEH-SABAOTH – Lord of Hosts (Angelic Armies)

EL ELYON – Most High

ABHIR – Mighty One

KADOSH – Holy One

SHAPHAT - Judge

EL ROI – God of Seeing

KANNA - Jealous

PALET - Deliverer

YESHUA - Savior

GAOL – Redeemer

MAGEN - Shield

EYALUTH - Strength

TSADDIQ – Righteous One

EL-OLAM – Everlasting God

EL-BERITH – God of Covenant

EL-GIBHOR – Mighty God

ZUR – God our Rock

MELEKH - King

In the New Testament, the God of the Old Testament is revealed as God the Father, God the Son (Jesus Christ) and God the Holy Spirit. Three persons or personalities, and often referred to as One God because they are totally unified in all of what they say and do, in complete union and agreement with one another.

Mankind (that is, both men and women) can be described as a three-part being with a physical body, a spirit and soul. The body comprises our flesh and blood along with five physical senses, our spirit comprises our uniqueness in person and our personality, and our soul is comprised of our intellect, reasoning capability, our will and emotions. With roughly 7 to 8 billion people on earth, each of us are unique. No two persons are exactly alike. Twins might be similar, but they're not exactly alike. It's been said in time past, that our spirit and soul are so interwoven that the only thing that is capable of separating them is the word of God. One could say that our five physical senses interconnect with our soul and spirit. Our eyes are the windows into our spirit. Our spirit is commonly referred to as our heart or the heart of a person in modern language. There is a conscience within each of us that can be identified as the inner voice of our spirit. Whether we recognize this aspect of our being or not, for many of us it is an inner voice or a knowing inside that leads us into living right or doing wrong, doing good or doing evil, choosing to sin or not to sin, etc. The Bible has a lot to say about our conscience. It even reveals that it's possible to have a seared conscience to where the conscience is no longer capable of receiving the goodness of God.

Then there are thoughts that come to our mind that are also another voice within us. What may be difficult for many Christians is learning to distinguish between the good and bad thoughts, knowing good voices from the bad voices. It is true we do have our own thoughts, but we must be aware there are also the voices and thoughts from others, such as friends and family, acquaintances, and other people. They are also souls with spirits in body. Then there are voices and thoughts from our spiritual enemy as well as those referred to as familiar spirits that are familiar with how we have lived our life. They influence the lives of unbelievers, and unfortunately also influence many Christians who are unaware. The only way one can know how to separate the two, the good from the bad, and know the difference between them is to become familiar with the thoughts and voice of the Holy Spirit. When one becomes a student or disciple of the living word of God and Holy Spirit, one begins to know the Father, His word and His thoughts above all other thoughts. Believers should learn how to reject the bad from the enemy and receive the good from the Father and His word. The battlefield is in our mind. (2Corinthians 10:5) Mankind is mostly unaware of this part of our spiritual battle within each of us. They think all the thoughts that come to their minds are their own, but this is not true.

In Genesis, we read that God blessed Adam and Eve by commanding them to subdue and have dominion over all the living creatures, to multiply and fill this earth and gave them a gift, the capability with authority to rule and have dominion over this creation on earth. Imagine, even though the Creator is the rightful owner of all creation, His will and desire gave all authority and power over this creation to mankind. He did this as a friend would give a cherished valuable gift, not wanting or expecting anything in return. He even gave Adam and Eve the privilege, the right and the honor of creating other "images of God" – children in his own likeness. What an awesome God!

With Adam and Eve, God desired a personal everlasting relationship to fellowship with them and their generations thereafter. A free-will was given with the privilege to choose and speak their own words. In addition, this free-will was given to love one another and to love Him of their own choice, and not by compulsion, an imposed will nor by edict. Created with the ability to speak words allowed them to be creative like God. Not necessarily on the same level of being creative as God, but function in the likeness of God. Allow me to put this in some context, we currently live on a planet that is filled with "words." Pictures are created in our thoughts from "words." If we look all around us, everything we see, what we do and everywhere we go in this world are governed by and created with words. One simple example of this would be our roadway traffic and signage system. If names and words were not directing us where to go, where to stop or where to turn, we would be driving our cars in chaos. Another great example would be the laws that govern us. If we didn't have laws or "words" guiding societies in this earth, lawless criminal elements would run rampant, and anarchy would be the normal way of life. In fact, we're actually experiencing much of this lawlessness in society today. "Words" have creative power and authority, whether we realize it or not. Words create thoughts and pictures in our minds to communicate and to stir our imagination. There are even unbelievers alive today who fully understand the power of the spoken and written word that have an effect on the lives of people in the society around them.

Words can speak life or they can speak death. Proverbs 18:21 says the power of death and life is in our tongue. With words, we can speak to a person with gentleness, love and kindness and they would more than likely feel happy and joyful. On the other hand, we can also speak words of hate and cursing to a person, to the point of where it could influence the rest of their life. Words are powerful and they're creative. Jesus goes further with identifying this by saying our words are from within our heart (spirit). Even he said this of himself, "my words are spirit and they are life."

With angels, it is different. They were created as a different class of being. Angels are spirits, but they were not created for us to worship, to freely communicate with, or to have a relationship with. They're simply messengers who mainly serve God and those who will inherit salvation, who communicate His word and will at various times to His children and are heavenly warriors battling the devil and his cohorts. We will not cover the subject of angels, but maybe at another time or for another book, the Lord willing.

When God created the face of this planet and everything in it, it was absolutely perfect. God was so pleased with it, He saw that "it was good." We must understand and develop a proper view of God from this, that God is good and this is His nature. Anything He has ever done in the past and all that He will ever do now and all that He will ever do in our future is solely based on His goodness. God started this creation in His goodness and He is not evil, nor does He do evil. There was no sin, sickness or evil in the creation nor in the Garden. (Genesis 1 & 2) We must keep this in mind and also remember, Satan is the one who perverted this creation. (Genesis 3, Isaiah 14:12-15 & Ezekiel 28:12-18)

God is good and He is the essence of what love truly is, He is love. (1Corinthians 13 & 1John 4) This creation was given to man as a gift and it was intended for our enjoyment and pleasure. There were no weeds in the ground, no thorns on the bushes or trees, no sicknesses nor any diseases, no curse, no pain, no aging, no sin and no death. Everything was good! There was peace of mind and heart, true joy in spirit and a godly hope of expectation of God manifesting more goodness toward Adam and Eve. Why would they have hope? God had commanded them to be fruitful and to multiply. In hope, they were to expect the blessing of having children from their union as husband and wife.

Animals did not kill each other for food, all fruit was food for the animals, Adam and Eve. They were living in God's utopia. Adam and Eve walked in faith with God, peace in mind and heart, no worries or strife, no sorrow or pain, and their physical bodies could live forever. Ever wonder why our own bodies have the ability for self-healing with an immune system? The answer is that our bodies were originally intended to live forever. There was no sin and death at this time. Everything in the earth was filled with the life, the presence and love of God. The Bible doesn't reveal to us how long Adam and Eve were living in the Garden of Eden.

Now it's time for the sad part, God gave them instructions to keep the Garden, or to work it as gardeners and to have dominion over it as their home. He also told Adam, that of all the trees within the garden, they could eat of all their fruit, except for one. God said if Adam ate of this tree named, "the Knowledge of Good and Evil," that he would surely die. God did not mean dying only in the sense of physical death as we tend to think of dying. This death resulted in a physical death, and it also included dying in the spirit (his heart), a spiritual death. (Genesis 3)

The following defines the difference between the two deaths:

Physical Death – is when your physical natural body ceases to function and you (your spirit) no longer resides physically in your body.

Spiritual Death – is total, complete separation from God in your spirit, soul and body. 'Sin' is death and separation from the life of God. He created our spirits to be eternal. Our spirit can either be saved and eternally alive to God, or can be eternally dead based upon our sin and separation from God.

Adam and Eve were working in the garden near the forbidden tree. They were doing what they had been instructed to do, keeping and working the Garden. We are not sure how the serpent made his way into the garden, but he found a way to camp out in this tree and wait for them. Some would attempt to refer to him as a snake to describe him, but we are unsure, what this creature was specifically. It wasn't until later, after Adam had sinned, that God curses the serpent to crawl on his belly like a snake there-after. We also understand from reading, that this was Adam's first mistake in life. In that He didn't keep or defend his home properly. He could've taken dominion over the serpent and kicked him out of the Garden. We also know the serpent allowed himself to be possessed by Satan to verbally communicate with Eve. It's at this point in the Bible where most husbands get all upset or bent out of shape with their wives, they will point to this scripture to blame them for all of their troubles in life. Well, I have some news for the men, those who may be a little ignorant of what the bible actually says here – Adam was with her when she was deceived and they both ate of this tree (Genesis 3:6). Adam was responsible here. You can find this by reading this verse in the various English translations.

It's very difficult to imagine, that a perfect man as Adam was, that he would somehow either forget what God had told him, or in some way experienced the fear of losing his wife. Forgetfulness and fear would not have had a place in his character or being, having been made in the likeness of God. The Bible doesn't reveal these details, but Adam was there with Eve when he heard the serpent speak that once the fruit was eaten, they would be like God knowing good and evil. Adam should have recognized this deception immediately that they had been made in the likeness and image of God already and should've knocked that fruit out of her hand. He had been given the tools, the authority and dominion from God to command and kick that serpent out of there. One can only wonder why this deception was so difficult to resist. Speculation would only be guessing. None of us were there and we don't know what was in the heart and mind of Adam at this moment, only God knows.

But we must understand, this temptation could have been resisted and corrected. Adam had the right, the power, all the authority on earth and all of heaven to back him up to throw out the serpent, even while Satan was talking to Eve. Adam could and should have stopped it. Eve could have been saved without delay. But Eve was deceived and she did eat. She messed up not fully remembering when repeating the commandment. Satan recognized this by twisting what God had said. Adam was with her and he heard everything that was said, and he chose to not do anything against this deception. He knew the truth of God's instruction. He chose to disobey and he did eat with Eve. Adam's choice to disobey was not the same as being deceived. Disobedience is worse than being deceived; it's very much like committing treason. Adam broke spiritual law and made the choice to disobey the commandment of God, in the same manner that Lucifer had chosen

to defy and disobey God before Adam's creation.

Some church leaders may say it was God's sovereign will, or that He predestined mankind to fall. They have their doctrinal reasons for believing this, reasons I've considered, but are contrary to the word of God. I'll disagree from the Biblical viewpoint that the fruit of this tree was a test of obedience of their faith in God and His word. There are certain individual scriptures that may appear on the surface to imply predestination of a certain few, but we have to look at the whole Bible in context by not singling out an individual verse. God's heart and integrity regarding this creation was for men and women to thrive and succeed in their life and to prosper with God at their side, to be blessed with good things and have dominion over the earth. If He didn't want man to have dominion over the earth and to prosper, then that would make God a deceiver and a liar. You wouldn't need a devil if this were true. Unfortunately, there's too much human reasoning prevalent in the church today. God wanted man to thrive and multiply on earth without the trouble caused from sin. I'd go further and state that from the beginning God desired mankind to be firmly established without sin in the earth in order to resist the forces of Satan and to openly show Satan and his cohorts throughout eternity what they have missed out on, which is living in the goodness and presence of God forever. (My opinion based upon Ephesians 3:11)

God was grieved by man's choice and fall into sin and in turn it created a separation from Him. Think about it, we were created to be like Him, in His image. Nothing else in creation was given this privilege or honor. Here's what happened from Adam and Eve's disobedience. Through sin they lost their godly privileges and were transformed to be under submission to Satan. All of Adam's God-given dominion and authority now belongs to Satan, and he now has the right to use this authority and dominion over mankind on the earth. In fact, Adam's rights reached from this earth all the way into the throne room of heaven and it allowed Satan to regain the right to re-enter heaven again. This event grieved God so much we can read the scripture in Genesis 3:22 has a long pause sigh inserted at the end, in this He had to remove Adam and Eve from Eden in order to keep them from eating of the fruit on the tree of life, which would have resulted in them living forever in the sin condition without having a way of redemption out of their sin. Redemption or salvation would not have been possible if that were to happen. God reveals His mercy by removing Adam and Eve from Eden. From this point forward, their life and mankind in the future will be dominated by a sin nature in them having contrary evil thoughts of deceptions, evil and lies.

Adam's communication with God was different than what it was before the fall. Now he's limited to live by his five physical senses and his thoughts. Communication before the fall was not only verbally spoken, but it also had to include spirit to spirit communion or a connection through the Holy Spirit. Satan was now in control and he continues to this day to deceive men and women to live in sin and to do evil, always motivated to ultimately destroy God's creation. Men and women become blinded in their hearts and minds to the things of God because of this sin-nature. Today we see the evidence of men and women dominating and multiplying on the earth, but they are not doing it under

God's blessing, but under Satan's influence. We can see that the sin nature continues to be passed down in every generation. God had given the privilege to procreate other "images of God" to Adam and Eve, and He could not take back His word to start over.

So, what was God to do in this situation? God had given all his authority and rights on earth to Adam, but then Adam gave them to Satan through sin. God's integrity and his word are binding, He will not violate His word, and spiritual law cannot be broken. Once God has spoken His word and the word is given, then spiritual law has been established and His word cannot be annulled or removed. Although God has the power to do so, He just couldn't go back to the dust of the earth and create another man to start over. He didn't have the right to do that. Although, He owns the earth, He had given the whole thing to man. God is so full of honor and integrity, He had to honor what he had given in the creation and honor what had happened after sin entered in. Essentially, this left God on the outside looking in.

Well, God is not a loser and it is not part of his nature. He wanted His man back. He loves man and His creation so much that He wasn't about to allow Satan to win this war. God is God, He is always prepared, the perfect plan for our situation and condition that He revealed in Genesis 3 was implemented for man's redemption. But we know God has a serious problem here. He must do this legally. Remember, He cannot and will not violate his word and any spiritual law He has spoken or established. We will come back to this plan, but let's review what happened with Satan in the following paragraphs.

In reference to Lucifer before his fall to become Satan, scripture indicates he was one of the highest-ranking angels in heaven. He was called the anointed cherub to minister before God and His throne. It's not difficult to consider that he held this position of authority over many millennia prior to Adam's creation. It's possible it may have been over many millions of years, no one knows for sure. Scripture implies he served God perfectly for an exceedingly long time under the anointing and with the authority God had given to him. He's been around a very long time. We do know he was an extremely beautiful angel, full of wisdom and apparently created with musical instruments built directly into his being. He walked in the presence of God and among the fiery stones on the mountain of God. One scripture implies that Lucifer may have had some level of authority on the earth as well, prior to our creation. (Ezekiel 28)

Lucifer may have been the musical worship minister in heaven before his fall. As a side note, look at all the distractions available in this life where he has influence. Things he has infiltrated through music, computers, cell phones, internet, social media, television and the entertainment industries, etc. Some would try to argue that not everything in this world is influenced by Satan. But one only has to consider the depravity, or how debased, or consider the depth of degradation that's in our society and in this entire world. This is mentioned as something to think about. Maybe there is a very real reason Satan is identified by Jesus and the apostles as the god of this world. Jesus warns us that we should be on the watch and alert regarding the influences we allow into our hearts and minds as we occupy this world. Lucifer became proud in his beauty, he basically became a "legend in his own mind" (self-centered, arrogant, proud) and chose to commit treason. He perverted his wisdom and the angelic anointing given to him from God to create sin. Therefore, there is no redemption for him and the fallen angels. Lucifer became the original author of sin and death; Jesus identified him as the father of all lies. It's difficult to fathom with human reasoning, that while Lucifer was in heaven and performing his service, that over a long period, he mastered deception so well, he was able to deceive and fully persuade one-third of the angels in heaven, leading a revolt to defy God in an attempt to take God's throne.

Lucifer was so good at deception that he had even deceived himself in his own wisdom to believe that a created being could possibly conquer his creator. The revolt itself didn't last long. Lucifer and his cohorts were defeated, stripped of their heavenly power and authority and cast out of heaven. His name was changed to Satan, he and his cohorts were abolished from heaven. An angel of God who had it all, living and walking in the goodness, love and presence of God for so many years, decides on his own that he should be God. To borrow a line from a popular movie, "...he chose poorly..."

Don't be too surprised, the same thing has happened many times on earth as well. All we have to do is consider the example of Judas Iscariot. Judas had the privilege, honor and a high office in the earthly ministry of Jesus. Judas witnessed Peter declaring Jesus was the Son of God, and heard Jesus declare that the Father had revealed that to Peter. Judas himself went on and in three years he participated in the ministry of Jesus through His authority by preaching the message, by healing the sick and the casting out demons. Yet, later on, at the covenant table of the Lord (the Passover), Judas chose to follow the promptings and deceptions of Satan in order to betray the Lord. It appeared to Judas that Jesus was not living up to his expectations. Like the other disciples, Judas also expected Jesus to set up God's kingdom on earth as the rightful king and Messiah to Israel. To the disappointment of Judas, near the end of his earthly ministry Jesus had been talking about being delivered over to the Gentiles to be killed. Judas must not have liked what the Lord was telling them.

While Jesus ministered on the earth, he mentioned to His disciples that he saw Satan cast out of heaven to the earth as lightning. This occurred before our creation. God didn't create Lucifer to be evil nor does He use the devil to teach lessons in life. God creates good things, not evil. Jesus Himself said if we see Him, we have seen the Father. To the disciples this meant that if they watched Him, heard Him and lived with Him, they were experiencing and hearing the Father in their presence. Because Jesus only did and spoke what the Father showed Him. The very nature and character of the Father is revealed in the Gospel accounts. The love that is in God the Father is revealed in the love chapter of 1st Corinthians 13. The fruits of the Spirit in Galatians chapter 5 are the attributes of God. In chapter 1 of Hebrews, it says Jesus is the express image of the Father. This means if you were to look at Jesus, his attitude, his actions, all that he is, we would see the Father in Him. What did Jesus do while on earth? He destroyed the works of the devil, healing ALL who were sick, diseased, lame, blind, deaf, mute and raised the dead, just to name a few. (Acts 10:38) Father God doesn't create evil, nor was it His will for Lucifer to change. Lucifer made his own choice, of his own free-will.

Just to be fair in this narrative and in response to those who believe God creates evil, please allow the following to explain the judgements of God noted in the Old Testament from a New Testament perspective. There's an unfortunate word usage in the KJV of the Bible found in Isaiah 45:7 where it appears to indicate that God does create evil. But, in the light of many other scriptures and other translations, this cannot be so. For instance, another translation of this scripture in the NKJV, the verse describes this as 'He creates calamity.' In Young's literal version, the verse describes 'He's preparing evil.' If we look up the meaning of the word evil, it simply means bad. In reading some commentaries of this scripture, it's noted as an unfortunate usage of the words selected. The word 'creates' implies doing a work of evil, this can't be so. The best way to consider the proper context of this one verse is to not look at anyone verse by itself, read the chapters and the verses in the context and history of its writing in order to get a grasp of what's happening. This scripture was written during a time of disobedience. When God's people chose to obey Him, they were a blessed people under the old covenant law. But, when God's people chose to not obey Him, He lifted His hand of protection and passed judgement that allowed the devil and the surrounding nations, or their enemies to defeat them and drag them into slavery. With this perspective, God judged which prepared the calamity when the nation of Israel had refused to repent of their sins. This happened repeatedly in the Old Testament. In the context of the entire Bible, God is not evil and does not create evil.

The Apostle John wrote the letter of 1 John to believers in the early years of the church in need of reassurance and encouragement because of the doctrinal conflicts they were having to deal with. John confirms with complete assurance and unshakable resolve that as a personal witness to the events of the Word of God manifesting on earth, he states "God is light, in Him is no darkness at all." (NKJV)

We also find in the book of Job where Elihu is revealing Job's error and God's character and justice in Chapter 34, and states in verses 10-12 (NKJV) –

> "Therefore listen to me, you men of understanding: Far be it from God to do wickedness, and from the Almighty to commit iniquity. For He repays man according to his work, and makes man to find a reward according to his way. Surely God will never do wickedly, nor will the Almighty pervert justice."

Considering the context of the verse in Isaiah, when compared with the blessings and curses listed in Deuteronomy 28, God can make things good in our life when we are living in obedience to the faith. On the other hand, if we are living in disobedience to the faith, in sin and unbelief, then we will have calamity and distress in our life from the enemy. If God has passed judgement in our life because we have refused to repent of sin or we've chosen to walk in disobedience, it's not because He's randomly choosing to be mean to us. We need to point our own finger directly back in our own direction for being the one who is choosing to do wrong and live in the bad situations and the poor choices we've made in life. He is always right and good. Remember, in the New Testament (Romans 2:4), it is His goodness that leads us to repentance (a choice of changing of our mind and direction in life) out from under the dominion of sin (Romans 6;14) to live for Christ free from sin and to live in the will of God. It also says to be mindful of both the goodness and the severity of God (Romans 11:22). He is gracious and merciful, but he is also right and just in all His works and judgements.

Another example is given in Exodus when God was instructing Moses regarding the Passover meal in Egypt. Initially, it appears that God is doing the striking when God says in the following verse –

Exodus 12:13 (NKJV) Now the blood shall be a sign for you on the houses where you are. And when I see the blood, I will pass over you; and the plague shall not be on you to destroy you when I strike the land of Egypt.

In this verse it does appear that God will do the striking. This may have an appearance of evil or bad happening, but we must remember that God is also a jealous God. He has passed judgement on the Egyptians and their gods and instructing the protection for His people. Now, let's look a little closer at a verse a little further down in the same chapter which sheds more light on the previous verse –

Exodus 12:23 (NKJV) For the LORD will pass through to strike the Egyptians; and when He sees the blood on the lintel and on the two doorposts, the LORD will pass over the door and not allow the destroyer to come into your houses to strike you.

Allow this to become clear in your understanding, based upon the second verse, God is passing judgment on the Egyptians. When He does, God's judgement allows the destroyer to destroy. God is not doing the destruction. He is passing judgement which allows or permits it to happen.

In a final example on how God judges, read the book of Job sometime. For time sake, it's not possible to review all 40 or so chapters. All we need to do is ask ourselves a couple of simple questions. When reading the first few chapters in Job, was God responsible for destroying Job's children, marriage, health and livelihood? The obvious answer is no. The evil one, Satan, did the destruction. Job may not have known who Satan was at this time. Near the beginning of the book, Job judged for himself and identified the reason for the destruction that came upon him. We will expand on Job in a following chapter of "why."

Chapter 2 – Who am I? (What's my purpose?)

Some theologians have suggested there may be a large timeline gap in the history of the creation between Genesis 1:1 to verse 2 and admittedly I lean in this direction of scriptural understanding. Scientific and archeological evidence has also created speculation that the climate of this earth was much different in the beginning of our creation. It may have very well been the time when dinosaurs roamed on the earth. Given the evidence, this could have also been the time when Lucifer and his cohorts were cast down out of heaven. The battle, the destruction and devastation could have been so massive that the whole earth became dark and void. This would align with the scripture in Genesis 1 saying "the earth was dark and void, without form." Think for a moment. Whenever there is light, warmth and life are associated with light. Whenever there is darkness, the warmth dissipates, and everything becomes cold. We don't know for sure, but the Ice Age could have occurred during this time. If there was life on earth in this period of time, life would have ceased to exist without light. Maybe the dinosaurs roamed the earth prior to the beginning of our creation. There's evidence all over this planet that suggests great temples were erected tens of thousands of years ago which may coincide with Lucifer's sanctuaries that are noted in Ezekiel 28 and were before our creation. In fact, the scientific big-bang theory of the universe sounds a whole lot like, "Let there be light! And it was..." In the grand scheme of things, does it really matter when all of this started? Men who don't know God and don't give regard to Him in the timeline of history are without faith. God set up this life on earth to be lived by faith in Him, not by what can or cannot be proven in the natural realm. There are some believers in the scientific community, but by and large, the scientific community continually shows their prejudice against any

God having involvement in this earth and in this creation. Little do they recognize they have been proving bits and pieces of evidence from the Bible. Evidence can be found, if one knows where to look. Yet, the Bible itself wasn't written to be a complete scientific and/or history book, although it does have evidence and history written in it. The focus of the Bible was written primarily to reveal the fall of man from God's goodness, the fallen rebellious condition of man's heart and God's plan of redemption through our Lord Jesus Christ.

What can be determined for sure is that mankind and science will never find their evidence and answers looking only with their natural physical senses, especially when they're only researching natural things for their evidence. The reality is, this physical life came from and exists because of what is unseen in the spirit, and that this spiritual life is behind it and holding it all together. Natural men may make advances in science and technology, but let's remember, all science is based upon men's natural-minded physical nature. Ever since the beginning of men's science, men have been trying to establish, theorize or prove there is no God. Sadly, they try to teach science and evolution as absolute truth. Well, it is sad for them because every time they have discovered a new thing, it really appears they've come closer to proving what God's word has already said. Man is notorious for continuously changing his viewpoint, his narrative and worldview.

When Satan had regained a foothold in God's creation through Adam's sin, this earth was also affected. The curse of sin was introduced in the earth in the physical realm. The curse of death, sicknesses, diseases, poverty, fear, hate, jealousy, strife, murder, lust, etc. just to name a few. The curse that was brought into the earth was thorns and thistles, extreme weather events, earthquakes, etc. In the book of Revelation, Satan is identified by another name, "the destroyer."

Since men are spiritually dead and under the curse of death, men and women begin to physically age and die. In Genesis, Adam and the early generations of men through the time of Noah lived a very long time. Almost a thousand years for some of them. Their physical bodies were originally created to live forever. They really didn't know how to physically die at first. Since man no longer had the life of God in them, their physical life span becomes shorter and shorter as time passes on. The physical effects of spiritual death with sin becomes more evident from generation to generation. All living animals turn on each other to kill for their food. They are no longer subject to man. Animals can be tamed, but they live in fear of us. An exception would be our domesticated pets that are not raised in the wild.

We also see that through all of this, God didn't completely reject mankind in his sin. Yes, He hates sin. Remember what was mentioned earlier, God loves mankind and His creation. He didn't leave them alone, even as they continued in their sin, In Genesis, He tried to work with fallen men and help them. When He did, they wouldn't listen to Him and He found that every inclination of man's heart and mind was intent on sin and to do evil. Men having Satan's sin nature in them, they only wanted to do what was right in their own eyes, living their life in the lust of their hearts in rebellion. So, God had to wait patiently until He could find men who would listen to Him and understand His goodness. From time to time, men and women would come along and follow God, commune or fellowship with Him in prayer and call on His name.

Let's review God's plan. Since man is the focus in the fall, he also must be the key in his redemption. The problem, man has Satan's sin nature in him, a man of sin cannot be used in this plan. As noted earlier, God could not go back to the dust of the earth to start over and create another man. But what could be done, that Satan didn't understand nor was he aware of, was that a second Adam could be created by the word of God. The spoken word that originally created Adam would have to be the same spoken word to create a new man. This would have to be a new man like Adam before he sinned. The only way God could do this was to get His word into this physical earthly realm by having men record it, write it down. In having it written down, this made it a legal right in the earth for God to create a new man in the flesh. And since men's hearts and minds were continually intent on doing evil, God would have to wait patiently for several generations and even hundreds of years before He could find men who would listen to Him and receive His word.

In the Old Testament, God found several men, but one in particular stood out, a man named Abram. God blessed him richly and made him the father of a nation. Later his name was changed to Abraham; we know his descendants as the nation as Israel today. God also found other men in this nation, several kings and prophets from different generations that would listen to Him to write down his words of hope for their deliverance from sin and gave them a promise that a future man, a messiah, would come to deliver them from their enemies and from their sin. God had them write down laws and commandments ("words") so they could know right from wrong, walk-in obedience, be blessed with prosperity and health, to walk in His ways and understand what sin would do to them.

The reason it took so long to get His word into the physical realm of this world was because of Satan's resistance and the hardness of men's heart. Remember, God is on the outside looking in. Legally then, and unto this day, He has to be invited here by men. When men call upon His name and to Him in prayer, this gave Him the right to come and intervene on the behalf of His children. He doesn't force Himself or impose His will on people. He's given us a free-will. As the rightful creator, owner and possessor of the earth, He could impose but He won't. He will not violate the integrity of the word He has spoken. Unfortunately, there were not very many men in the Old Testament who would listen to God. Some of Israel's generations would serve and listen to God. When they obeyed, they were a strong, blessed and rich nation. When they disobeyed, they were taken into slavery and severely punished, many times.

Here's one example, just because God said, "Do not commit adultery", as one of the Ten Commandments, it was given not because God didn't want anyone having any fun! It is wrong because adultery will kill you spiritually and physically. Sin may be pleasurable for a time in our life, but sin will always lead to destruction. The book of Proverbs describes extensively what happens to people when adultery is pursued. The reason adultery is wrong is that the solemn vow in marriage covenant was to be a binding commitment in love, to be highly esteemed (most-valued) and honored. In the eyes of God, it is a binding contract recognizing the male and female together as a couple as one flesh. Marriage was intended to bring pleasure and joy to the couple in spirit, soul and body. A dedication of unqualified committal with each other in a family relationship, then procreate and raise godly children. No matter how a psychologist may try to twist or sugar-coat this, adultery destroys not only the persons involved, but it also destroys families, hardens the hearts of the children in the marriage and others around them. Now, let's thank God for His provision of grace and mercy, for forgiveness and the gift of repentance through Christ who has delivered us from the dominion of sin.

For those who are still pondering the previous paragraphs, questioning and pondering the idea that God doesn't force himself or impose His will on anyone, some may disagree on this comment. And, rightly so, let's review this further because there are scriptures that discuss the Pharaoh of Egypt during the deliverance of the children of Israel from their bondage and slavery. In Exodus 9:16 and in Romans chapter 9, there are scriptures basically stating that God used Pharaoh to reveal His power for His name to be declared in all the earth. On the surface, it may look like God didn't give Pharaoh much of a chance in this situation. In fact, in Exodus 9:16, there is no statement here that God chose

Pharaoh to resist Him. Given the nature of this man was shown to be stubborn and rebellious and he wouldn't be someone who would listen to God for his own good. We must keep in mind, all of Egypt's Pharaohs were raised worshipping other gods along with believing they were gods themselves.

We can believe that God influences human affairs so that such a person would be on the throne of Egypt at the time one was needed in the fulfillment of His plan; but we cannot believe that Pharaoh would not have been permitted to repent and become submissive had he made the choice to cease being rebellious. It was purely a personal choice with him as it is with all mankind. God gave him choice of his own free-will. What's telling is that before Moses meets Pharaoh, God reveals to Moses He will harden the heart of Pharaoh in Exodus 4:21. Then when Moses meets Pharaoh the first time it is Pharaoh (Exodus 5:2) who is the first to resist God by saying,

> " Who is the Lord, that I should obey his voice to let Israel go? I do not know the Lord, nor will I let Israel go." (NKJV) God didn't harden Pharaoh's heart at this point. God allowed him to make the initial choice of which way this was going to go."

It is plain to see the Egyptians were not turning to God during all of the hardship and loss through all of the plagues brought upon them. They were not a people turning to God in these events. In fact, later and instead of turning to God at the end of the plagues, they gave their gold, silver and possessions to the Israelites and begged them to leave their land to be rid of them. Here is a lesson in this, when you mess around hurting God's covenant people, He takes it personally. The accuser and abuser of God's people are going to have a very harsh meeting with God and God will be the one who will remain standing at the end of that brief meeting. This is a good example of how God knows those who are His and those who will not choose to be His.

In another proof of God's grace and mercy in the Old Testament, He went out of His way to provide a substitute for the death penalty of sin. He made provision to incorporate the process of animal sacrifice with the shedding of blood for the covering of man's sin. Blood sacrifice using animals was instituted as a ministry service for His people. The annual offering and covering couldn't take away the guilt of the sins committed, but it provided a way for His people to remain in contact with God. This was truly the grace and mercy of God. We will expand on this in a subsequent chapter.

So, over a period of one thousand five hundred years, God finally gets enough of His "word" into this physical realm written down. It had to be written in such a way that mere men couldn't fully comprehend it, nor could Satan. God didn't want to reveal His plans to His arch enemy. When God finally gets enough of His written word into this earth, He looks to a young woman named Mary, a virgin. The archangel Gabriel was sent by God to speak God's message that she was highly favored and would give birth to a son and name him Jesus. Though fearful at first, she chooses to accept God's word and His will for her life.

Before continuing, let's look at a side note to reveal some physical evidence –

On the cellular level, Medical Science has proven and concluded that every cell in man's physical body regenerates itself every seven years. In other words, our human body should not be capable of dying. There is no natural or honest medical reason of "what, how and why" physical aging and death occurs in our bodies. The Bible identifies that death is caused due to the curse of sin.

Medical Science has also proven and concluded the male human sperm contains the seed for his children's blood. The physical life of the body is in our blood, the seed of our blood always comes through our fathers.

Read the following carefully, when Mary accepted the word of God for this event, that spoken word from God became the seed in Mary's womb. The Holy Spirit hovered over her with the creative power of

God the same as when He hovered over the face of the earth in the book of Genesis. She became pregnant with Jesus. As God spoke his word to create Adam, he again speaks his word in the earth to create Jesus in her womb. Jesus is conceived. Not with the blood of men, but with the blood from God the Father. Jesus was born with sin-free blood in lieu of sin-tainted blood. This is why the Gospel of John starts chapter 1 with the phrase, "In the beginning was the Word and the Word was with God, and the Word was God" (NKJV) Later in verse 14," And the Word became flesh and dwelt among us." (NKJV) As mentioned before, God had kept this plan of redemption hidden from man and Satan. That's the reason for sending the angel directly to Mary. Her pregnancy wasn't announced to the world, but quietly at her house. When His birth occurred, then it was announced out in the fields where shepherds were watching their flocks at night. Since Satan is limited to man's realm on earth, he and his cohorts are not omnipresent and he didn't become fully aware of where Jesus was located, though he knew something was happening. Satan didn't really think that God could create Jesus as he had done with Adam. Some thirty years after Jesus was born, Satan becomes fully aware when, at the baptism, he heard God in Heaven declare to John the Baptist that – "This is my beloved Son, in whom I am well pleased!" (NKJV)

Directly after being baptized, Jesus, full of the Holy Spirit, goes into the wilderness alone. He does this because He needed to pass the test of Adam before he could begin his earthly ministry. He begins the journey by fasting and praying, and continues over a period of 40 days. Usually, the average person can fast or not eat up to 2 or 3 weeks with no serious harm, but 40 days of fasting is life threatening to the human body. People can die from attempting this. Jesus didn't do this to try and show off, He was making sure that His fleshly body was under His spiritual control at all times and it was His way of checking himself for self-control. But He had to take this to the breaking point of true weakness before standing against the coming temptations. After 40 days, Satan comes to him to tempt him the same way he tempted Adam and Eve, with food. Satan said, "If you are the Son of God, turn these stones into bread".(NKJV) Jesus was desperately starving and sorely tempted, but He resisted the devil by using God's word saying, "You shall not tempt the Lord your God." (NKJV) Satan then tempted Him two more times, but to no avail. Jesus wins the battle by standing on God's word. Jesus proved that a man filled with the Holy Spirit and full of God's word can conquer and resist temptation. Please understand, he didn't conquer Satan by using any of God's supernatural powers. The epistle to the Philippians says He left all His Godly privileges behind in heaven. Jesus, the man, won this battle filled with the Holy Spirit as His helper. Satan now knows he is going to be in a battle for his dominion during Jesus ministry, and he was going to continue waging spiritual war against Jesus.

From here on in the New Testament we can see the second Adam, Jesus walking the earth, tempted to sin all the time, but he chooses to resist sin. He chooses to do God's will over his own will. The bible says that he joyfully emptied himself of any and all his godly privileges, humbling himself and came to earth to be a servant. (Philippians 2:5-8) He did this to not only show us what Adam should have done in the Garden, but He also shows us how He went about in His daily life intent on conquering the works of the devil – sin, sicknesses, diseases with deliverances from demonic possession, just to name a few. (Acts 10:38) He does this as a man, not as "the Son of God." He even calls himself the Son of Man numerous times to confuse the religious leaders and the people. In His earthly ministry, He found men to disciple, to learn His ways as He had learned from His Father God.

As Jesus followed God's will and taught God's word to the people, Jesus openly showed God's good will, love and pleasure by serving people in healing the sick, causing the blind to see, the deaf to hear, healing the mentally disabled, the lame and paralyzed, healed those who had leprosy, healed others with terminal diseases, cast out demons from many who were possessed and raised the dead back to life. God revealed himself through Jesus, and Jesus revealed the Father to the people. By showing His grace and mercy, loving on His people. Our natural minds can barely grasp the magnitude of these miracles. The disciple John wrote at the end of his gospel account (John 21:25),

> "And there are also many other things that Jesus did, which if they were written one by one, I suppose that even the world itself could not contain the books that would be written." (NKJV)

Jesus ministered this way for three and a half years. Think about this for a moment, Satan and his cohorts ushered in the curses of sin, sickness, disease and death. These are used by him to destroy lives and bodies. In our so-called modern times, natural men who do not acknowledge God, generally think that we have to live with these curses because they are a part of our natural physical life. Some think there is no hope of escape. Others may believe that if they eat the right foods and/or exercise regularly, they will have a chance of living longer. There may be an element of truth to the eating and exercising part, but those who are not living for God in their lives are not promised to have a long life on earth. Living in a world system that is dominated under Satan's control and influence, accidents will happen and they regularly do happen. But with the help of the Holy Spirit, believers can have a godly hope of deliverance through a lifestyle of faith that is free from the burden of sin. A hope of divine health, a covenant of healing and a long-life on the earth. There is hope of prospering and being successful in this earthly life. The hope of our bodies being resurrected from the corruption of sin and death to a new life with Him. This hope is received through the Lordship of Jesus Christ in the life of each believer.

When God healed someone through Jesus, it was a conquest of Satan. Jesus as a man never sinned and never failed in His ministry.

Jesus never allowed Satan to win. Where Adam had failed, Jesus overcame. Jesus had the capability to sin and was tempted as we are, but He chose not to sin. He lives to please God in every way. Through the new birth, He enables and empowers believers with the ability to be free and to overcome sin in this world.

Now Satan realizes he has a serious problem. Men and women are flocking to Jesus because of his good message of God's kingdom and because of all the miracles He is doing. Satan is losing. Jesus is winning. So, Satan sets out to destroy Jesus and he does this through the ruling class in the religious hierarchy of the day. As we know the Jewish religion was based upon God's laws, but their hearts were far from esteeming and honoring God. They did observe the word of God and the covenant laws and other ceremonial practices, but their observation was through ritual practice and their own interpretation. They had added burdensome rules and regulations onto the word of God, presuming they were correctly interpreting the word of God. One example given was when Jesus rebuked the religious leaders over one of the 10 commandments that says,

> "Keep the Sabbath, to keep it holy, as the Lord your God commanded you. Six days you shall work, but the seventh day is the Sabbath. (day of rest from work)." (Exodus 20:8 – NKJV)

The Sabbath was one day of the week to set aside to rest from the daily job and remember the good things of God, to study and meditate on His word, much like Sundays are set up for going to church. The religious hierarchy took this further, by saying that no work could be done at all and in their interpretation, they added onto what God said. Jesus was against this. He realized the religious hierarchy was not teaching God's word the way it should have been. Jesus loved people, including the religious leaders, but we can see a small part of how He hated the religion and tradition inside of them. Many times, Jesus healed people on the Sabbath. Because of this, He got Himself in more hot water all the time with the religious leaders because He did it on the Sabbath. They considered healing on the Sabbath day as work! But Jesus kept on doing what pleased the Father. It was God's goodness and His will that Jesus heals people on the Sabbath. It's a wonder, why would they be so upset with someone being healed or set free? Jesus and these religious leaders had many loud confrontations during his ministry. The religious leaders refused to see Jesus as their Messiah. This was due to the hardness of their hearts and being so wrapped up in their traditions. Over time, they begin to plot and find a way to kill Him. Satan finally found his accomplices who would do his will.

As previously mentioned, the penalty for sin is death. Mankind deserves death for sin. The One who was created like Adam knows He will have to spiritually and physically die in order to redeem men from Satan's dominion and from sin. Jesus knew this. Later in His ministry, Jesus begins to tell His disciples that He must die, but He didn't give them the reason just yet. Toward the end of His earthly ministry the religious leaders were looking for any kind of accusation to kill Him. As noted earlier, Judas Iscariot was the treasurer in Jesus ministry. Early on in Jesus ministry, Judas was probably excited with the prospect of serving and following Jesus in the ministry works of healing and deliverance, as well as preaching the Kingdom of God and repentance from sins. But, like everyone else, he was looking for the Messiah who would set up God's kingdom on earth delivering the nation of Israel from the bondage of Roman rule. I'd suspect later on that he became distressed with talk of Jesus dying. In addition, it had become known among the disciples that he would steal money from the ministry for his own uses. So, we can see that Judas actions were revealing his heart was not right before the Lord. Judas ended up being the one betraying Jesus to the religious leaders. Once they got a hold of Jesus. They attempted to bring false charges and accusations against Him. Jesus allowed this to happen because He knew the price to redeem man was through his sacrificial death. God not only loved mankind, so did Jesus. Jesus was willing to sacrifice himself for us. During His trials, he didn't defend Himself. He hardly uttered a word. Even when He was being mocked, spat on, beaten and bruised by the soldiers, Jesus remained silent.

When Jesus was brought before Pilate, the Roman Governor, He questioned Jesus about these accusations the Jews had made. Jesus said His kingdom was not of this earth. Pilate concluded Jesus didn't deserve death, but because of the politics between the Romans and the Jewish kingdom, in addition to the religious leaders screaming for death, Pilate gives in to the desires of the riot. Jesus, an innocent sinless man was to die the death of a criminal. Death on a cross. We cannot imagine the pain Jesus had to endure. The bible says Jesus was so marred and beaten we wouldn't recognize Him as a man. They led Him to be crucified. When crucified, Jesus hung on that cross for six hours. This was in the middle of the day. While He hung there, the sky turned black. Not with dark rain clouds and not with a solar eclipse. The reason the sky turned black while Jesus was hanging there was all of mankind's sins from the past, the present and the future were being laid on Jesus. In addition to this, every curse of all sickness and all disease which were known and unknown to man were placed upon Him. He became sin with our sin on that cross. He bore all of this in his body and became cursed with our curse. When this happened, God turned his face away from Jesus and couldn't look at him. The bible says that God is light. It was so dark during this event that the light would not shine. The Roman soldier who had performed countless other crucifixions became so horrified at the sight of Jesus and the darkness, he shouted, "Surely, this is the Son of God!" We can't even imagine the sight of what Jesus looked like and this moment in time.

Finally, when Jesus neared His end on the cross, He cried out, "Father, forgive them for they don't understand what they have done!" Then said a moment later, "Father, into your hands I commit my spirit."

(Luke 23 paraphrased) Then, His body physically died. But the Father didn't take His spirit. God had turned His face from Jesus because of the sin that was placed on Him. Satan and his cohorts took Him. Jesus became spiritually dead, separated from the Father. For three days He was separated from His Father God in the heart of the earth. In that time His body was placed in a tomb. All His followers had deserted Him in fear of their own lives. Mary His mother had watched all of this. We know her heart had to be grieving over this, she didn't understand what was happening. But there is good news that came out of this, believe it or not. Jesus willingly did this for us. He allowed this. Some might not understand and say, how could this be good news to us?

Satan didn't think God could do what He did. Satan had missed one spiritual law. Satan is only allowed to take an unrepentant sinner to hell legally. He broke spiritual law by murdering a man who never sinned, a man of innocent blood. Satan spilled God's blood through the hands of men. This is the plan Satan never knew about. If he had known about this, he never would have killed Jesus. But in murdering Him, this satisfied the spiritual death penalty of Adam's sin. Jesus became the final blood sacrifice to satisfy the penalty of sin and paid the price for all of us. This is why He's referred to as the spotless Lamb of God. In spirit, Jesus battled Satan and his cohorts, preached to the fallen angels held in the prison of hell during the three days while his body laid in the tomb. When the penalty was paid and satisfied on the third day, the hand of God released Jesus' soul and spirit from the grip of hell and death. God resurrects Jesus from the dead. Jesus conquers Satan, He takes the keys of death and hell. Jesus rises from physical death to a new life in His glorified body. Death has no power or authority to hold onto Him anymore. This is good news!! A resurrected man has conquered God's arch enemy. From this point onward, Jesus sets a new course in mankind's future. For those who believe can now have a new living hope for their future!

When the disciples heard about the tomb being empty and that Jesus was alive, even they had a hard time believing it. Then, Jesus surprised them all by instantly appearing in the midst of them while they were all together. He didn't even open the door; He walked through the closed door into their room. He just "showed up." They were all frightened and in fear. They thought He was a ghost at first. He knew they were in fear of Him and having a hard time believing, He says to them, "Handle me! A spirit does not have flesh and bone as you see me have." (Luke 24 paraphrased) Then after touching the holes in His feet and hands He sat down with them and joined them for dinner to calm them down and teach them about what had just happened and explain why it had to happen the way it did. He opened their understanding to the Old Testament prophets and the Psalms. Then He surprises them again and leaves the same way He came in. Talk about a glorified resurrected body! His body doesn't have any blood. His innocent blood was shed for our sins, now His veins are now filled with the power and glory of God! Now, His body lives forever. Jesus appears to the disciples several more times. First, he appeared to the eleven, then to the seventy-two and finally to several hundred disciples. Now men can have hope in a hopeless world. God the Father accomplishes His redemption plan through Jesus.

At this point it would be apropos to interject additional knowledge of why I believe what I wrote in the previous three paragraphs that make partial reference of what happened from the cross to the throne. In my heart, there are not enough words in the English language that even come close to expressing all of what He is, who he is, and all of what He has done to free us from this sin nature. We may continue to study and learn for the remainder of our lives on earth, but we will only know in part until the day of the Lord's return. Just simply comprehending how high He really was in the beginning with God, then to understand how low He had to descend from heaven to become flesh and blood, choosing to set aside and not use His Godly privileges to become a man is nearly indescribable, since heaven remains a mystery to us. We get glimpses of heaven through the word, but by and large, it's a mystery. Then topping it off, He chose to become cursed on the cross with our sin and to die in our place for the redemption of sinful man. His faith in God, the humility and willingness to follow through with taking our sin is beyond comprehension.

There is a doctrinal belief that is taught that Jesus only died in the flesh and didn't die in spirit. In addition, that He didn't go into hell, but only went to the place commonly referred to as Abraham's Bosom. This doctrine basically states that because of the Deity of Jesus Christ, Him being one with the Father, that He has never been separated from the Father. There have been pastors in my past who adopted this position. When they preached this from the pulpit, this appeared strange to me at the time. In my opinion, this doctrine appears to conflict with a quite a number of scriptures. I believe there was a brief time when there was a separation between the Lord Jesus and the Father. This has been a hotly debated item within our circles for many years.

I would simply offer that during the earthly ministry of Jesus, He prophesied that like Jonah, He would be three days and nights in the heart of the earth. And while He was on the cross, He cried out, "My God, My God, Why have you forsaken me?" (Matt. 27: 46 NKJV) Jesus Himself knew the moment when the Spirit of God left Him on the cross. This coincides with the account of the woman with the issue of blood when she touched Him for healing. The word says He sensed the power of the Spirit flow to the woman. According to Paul in his second letter to the Corinthian church, he stated that Jesus was made to be sin. This agrees with Isaiah 53. Our sin separated Him from the Father.

Most Christian people will accept the fact that Jesus died physically on the cross. But there are some who reject that Jesus had to also experience spiritual death as well. They lean toward relying on the scripture in 1 Peter 3:18. But in reading this scripture, it has to be read in context with Jesus preaching to the disobedient spirits in prison given in verses of 19 through 22. The 'spirits in prison' were not the same as those who were held in Abraham's Bosom. Though verse 18 states He was 'put to death in the flesh' but it goes on to further say He was 'made alive by the Spirit'. (NKJV)

Sin is spiritual death and simply means separation from the life of God. In Psalms 16:10 and in Jonah Chapter 2, the verses here are prophetic of our Lord crying out from Sheol. In Acts 2:24, Peter preaching on the Day of Pentecost said that God raised Jesus up 'having loosed the pains of death.' The word 'pains' is plural. Then a moment later in verse 31, Peter confirms Psalm 16, that upon the resurrection of Jesus, His soul was not left in Hades, nor did His flesh see corruption. This was fresh in Peter's mind from when Jesus had opened up the Prophets and the Psalms to His disciples when He appeared to them shortly after His resurrection.

Then, there is a portion of 1Timothy 3:16 (NKJV) that states, He was "…. Justified in the Spirit…" A person is unable to be justified without having first been unjustified or unrighteous. He was made to be sin on the cross having been made sin with all of our sins. That is the sins of the flesh, the sins of the mind and the sins of the heart. Being made sin required Him to go into hell to pay the full price for three days and nights. The good news is He was not left there. Father God raised Him from the dead, and has exalted Him to sit at His right hand. The Lord's prayer to the Father in John 17:5 (NKJV) was answered by the resurrection, "And now, O Father, glorify me together with Yourself, with the glory which I had with You before the world was."

In John 1:1, it is true that Jesus is the manifested Word of God, He was God and was with God from the beginning. This doesn't necessarily mean or imply that Jesus has never existed apart from the Father. We need to remember that though He was God, He chose to empty Himself of those Godly privileges and He operated as a man on the earth. This doesn't minimize Him nor take away from acknowledging His Deity. While on earth, He called Himself the Son of Man. He also had help from the Helper once He was baptized in the Jordan river.

By writing this, I know there will be some doctrinal and theological differences with others within my world or sphere of influence. I understand we are all on many different levels of life experiences and knowledge. Hopefully, we can fulfill the Lord's command of 'love one another' despite these differences.

God's plan continues. Men and women now have a choice to continue to live in sin and be like their father Satan, or to be set free from their sin in a newness of life that comes through Jesus Christ. Those who choose to be born-again are placed in right-standing with their Heavenly Father as if they had never sinned. This was the free gift of God to all who believe. While on earth, Jesus said "For God so loved the world that He gave His only Son, that whosoever believes in Him, shall not perish, but have everlasting life" (John 3:16 paraphrased) and in another place He said, "I am the Way, the Truth and the Life. No one comes to the Father except through Me" (John 14:6 paraphrased). God's word says in other places that if we confess Jesus as Lord of our life and believe in our heart He was raised from the dead, and those who call on the name of the Lord we will be saved. When men and women recognize that Jesus is the way to heaven, make their choice to follow Him, have relationship with Him and the Father, by walking and living their life in His love and His word, their dead spirit comes alive in Him. God adopts them as His own children. This is why the bible calls Jesus the "first-born" from the dead among many brethren. As He was raised from the dead, we are also born again into a new life in Him. This is the heart of the gospel, the good news!

Satan continues to have more problems after he loses to Jesus and God the Father having raised Him from the dead. Jesus had told His disciples before He was crucified that He would not leave them as orphans, but would send them the Holy Spirit. He said that if He did not go back to the Father, the Holy Spirit could not come. After Jesus goes to heaven as the Son of God, on the day of Pentecost in the book of Acts, we see thousands coming to Christ being saved. This is when the ministry of the Holy Spirit began through the disciples, who became apostles during this time. What was Satan's problem here? Other "images of Jesus" are being created when men start making a choice to be saved, being born-again in Christ. The Holy Spirit came in power and was doing the works of Jesus through the hands and the lives of born-again men. The same good works and healings that Jesus ministered on earth are now being continued through the ministry of the Holy Spirit. This was God's good pleasure and His will since the fall of Adam, and it is His good pleasure and will continuing to this day.

Let's review a brief history lesson after the time of the New Testament. When the Holy Spirit burst onto the scene in the book of Acts shortly after the resurrection of Jesus, we read where thousands are born-again, turning to God and joining the church. As prophesied by Jesus, history has recorded the complete destruction of Jerusalem by the Roman empire in 70AD. A non-believing Jewish historian named Josephus recorded this event in his writings and he also acknowledges the life of Jesus of Nazareth before this destruction. After a couple hundred years, many millions of people became Christians in the Roman Empire. These people were not just church goers only on Christmas Sunday. They were true believers, born-again, spirit-filled Christians that would lay hands on the sick and the sick would recover! They received the same Holy Spirit that Jesus had received when He was baptized in the Jordan River. During this time of Christianity, the Roman Empire was at its peak. Christians were under extreme persecution from unbelievers, even to the point of physical death. It is my opinion; I don't believe this bothered them much. Because of what Jesus did, there was no longer a fear of death for most; they had a new hope of going to heaven free from sin and were glad to die in Jesus name and gave God great glory in martyrdom. Christianity continued to grow tremendously and for some time Satan and his cohorts couldn't figure out how to stop the growth of the church. But there did come a time in the third century when Satan and his kingdom apparently figured out a way to slow it down and twist the message of the gospel.

This is where the prophetic parable of Jesus started to become a reality in history, the parable of the wheat and the tares. (Read Matthew 13:24-30 and how Jesus explains this parable in Matthew 13:36-43) A tare is similar in appearance to wheat, but is considered an undesirable weed in the field of grain.

When Constantine became ruler of the Roman Empire, Christianity began to transition and change from being a persecuted church into a state religion. Under Constantine, whether he was a believer or not, he was considered by and large a good leader. He allowed for a tolerance of other religions within the state. By establishing the new state church system of Christianity, this enabled many good things to occur within the empire, the main items being the abrupt halt to crucifixions, all persecution of Christians and a new freedom of worship without fear of their lives, just to name a few. Heathen worship was tolerated and allowed to continue, but the practice of animal sacrifice to pagan gods was outlawed. Constantine believed in conversion of the heathen via evangelism that was

gradual, in lieu of by compulsion.

Once Constantine's son came into power and rule as well as subsequent successors, the state religion quickly became intolerant. Heathen conversion was progressing, but might have been too rapid for the health of the church. Christian emperors after Constantine accelerated the movement by issuing laws detrimental to heathen practices and beliefs. Heathen sacrifices and worship were forbidden, and observance was made a criminal offense. Not long after Constantine's reign his son ordered all idol worshippers to be given the death penalty along with the loss and confiscation of their property.

One of the negative observations about Constantine's reign and the church leaders after him in both the Catholic and Greek Orthodox churches, they began an attempt to identify various biblical locations in the land of Israel and the Egyptian Sinai Peninsula. One of their major mistakes was to identify a mountain as Mt. Sinai in the peninsula area, when evidence indicates it is actually located in northwest Arabia. The Apostle Paul said the mountain was located in Arabia in his letter to the Galatians. Several people have visited the mountain and recorded evidence on the site known today as Jabal-al-Lawz. I'm convinced this is the location. If you desire to know more about the historical evidence, I recommend reviewing videos, dvd's, and/or YouTube for Jim and Penny Caldwell's testimony of traveling to northwest Saudi Arabia and their discoveries and evidence of the Exodus, the Mt. Sinai area and the Split-rock location. Or review these on their website at https://www.splitrockresearch.org/. Another good reference to review is Tim Mahoney's video or dvd called "Patterns of Evidence."

After Constantine's reign, persecution of Christians appears to cease. Unbelievers didn't want to be put to death, so the easy thing to do was join the church and claim to be Christians as well. This action starts the degradation and dulling of the church body as a whole. Unbelieving religious leaders become prominent in the religious church hierarchy and Satan has found a way to deceive the church and its members for many hundreds of years. It is also during this time Satan convinces the religious leaders to gather up all the known letters (or books) of the Bible and have them locked up in monasteries. God's word says, "we are born-again by the imperishable word of God." When God's word was removed from the common people, the evidence implies, and from what little the history can reveal, many people were not being born-again. The people at that time didn't have a bible like we do today. The printing press hadn't been invented yet.

Prior to this, the New Testament letters of the time were continually passed around from church to church across the empire over those hundreds of years. All the churches would read these aloud to the common people to hear the Word of God and they would believe and live their daily lives according to the Word they heard. In Romans 10:17, "...faith comes by hearing the Word of God." Since there were synagogues available all over the empire, believers would also rely on the Old Testament scriptures for the revelation of Jesus Christ. Jesus said that those who hear the word of God (to keep it and do it), are compared to those who build their house on a solid foundation and when the storm (or storms of life) come, the house is immovable and safe. And those who hear the word of God and go their own path (choosing to do what is right in their own eyes) are compared to those who build their house on a sandy foundation and when the storm comes, it is destroyed and demolished.

When all of God's written word had been removed and stored in monasteries, very few people were experiencing the new birth. Only God knows who they were. Christianity became more of a life-less ritual, a religion to many. They stopped relying on the direction of the Holy Spirit and were doing what appeared to be right in their own eyes. Only the religious leaders could read and preach from the scriptures. Unfortunately, religion ruled in the earth for an exceptionally long time with the deception of Satan upon many unbelieving religious leaders. It's obvious none of this was God's plan nor His will. Scripture identifies God as the full expression of love and reveals His goodness. He's not, the Author of death; the bible clearly indicates He is the Author of life. God was not a part of this transition even though men may have stated many things in history were done in the name of God, they were not.

Men have done things in the name of God that were total abominations in His sight. One example, initially instigated by continual criminal harassment and death from Muslims upon Christians on their pilgrimages to Jerusalem and the Holy Land. What began as protection for pilgrimage soon developed into European

Crusades for conquest. Religious men attempted to free Jerusalem from Muslim control and re-establish God's kingdom on earth in the name of God. This again was not God's will, and He did not have His hand in this. That is why it failed miserably with a great loss of many lives.

During these dark times in our history, there were honorable believers; there were some who were stirred in their hearts by the Holy Spirit and by God's will to painstakingly translate and copy the locked-up letters of the New Testament. Many were caught and killed because it was against church doctrine to do this. Blood has been spilled over the ages in many attempts of getting the Word of God back into the hands of common people where the new birth and true growth in Christ could occur.

All of us remember other events like the Dark Ages and the Bubonic Plague. Why did these events occur? In my opinion it was due to God's word being locked up and men had lost sight of relying on God for His help. Satan was controlling these destructive events. The bible says, "God is light and in him is no darkness at all". We can see that when the light of God (or knowledge of God) is removed from the earth, this earth experiences dark times. In addition, millions died in the Bubonic plague. This was not God's will. This event had to have grieved Him tremendously.

As history progresses to the 14th and through the 17th centuries the Renaissance was under way. Historians tend to glorify this period of men's accomplishments because by all appearance, the Dark Ages had passed away and men were now exploring various art forms, intellectualism, and sciences in the so-called human enlightenment, which touched the whole European world. Also, during this time an interesting thing was happening, the religious church eased its tensions on translating God's word. The religious hierarchy in the church no longer believed God worked in the earth or in men anymore, as it was recorded in God's word. Well, they were wrong; they forgot that the

Holy Spirit was still here, working with believers. He never left His earthly ministry. He was and still is here and there were believers who were waiting for this day to occur. And when the religious church eased up, that is when the Holy Spirit moved on men's hearts to get the word translated.

In 1611 King James, the King of England had his interpreters translate the word into the English language and had it published. A compilation of 66 books and letters that had been written over a period of 1500 years were brought together under one binding for the common man. This was the spark. Now people have a way to read and hear the word of God in their common language again. The Church of England was started, although it was still deeply religious in nature, common men were beginning to get the message again, the good news of the gospel. Common men were being born-again by hearing the word of God. (1 Peter 1:23)

As the industrial revolution came along, printing presses were multiplying bibles for born again men of God to preach and teach the word of God, this time taking it all around the world. Through the 1800's and 1900's, God's word spread rapidly. Up to this day and hour, God's word is now going across this planet via satellite, TV and radio, reaching places where we are forbidden to physically go to. Satan is fighting a losing battle.

Now let's remember, God still has to honor what had happened in the Garden of Eden. He is still on the outside looking in. The spiritual law is that God has to be invited here when men call on His name in prayer. The bible says Satan is still the prince of power in the air and is the god of this world, or this world system. Satan still has influence and control here and continues to work in the sons and daughters of disobedience with the dominion that was given to him by Adam. Even though Jesus has defeated Satan, this spiritual law remains in effect. God has to be invited here by men and women who will receive Him into their lives. God will not reveal himself to sinful men and women who deny God exists, but He will reveal himself to people who choose to believe. God desires to be involved in every man and woman's life for their good and their benefit. But it is up to each man and woman to make the choice. God the Father and Jesus have done their part. And now there is additional help through the Helper (Holy Spirit) who is here for us to overcome this worldly system and the sin.

Since we live in this sinful earth, whether we are born again or not, "evil" happens to both good and bad people, "accidents and death" happen to good and bad people," sickness, disease and death" happens to both good and bad people. Whether evil and sin are directly caused by Satan himself, or through other evil sinful men and women, things are going to happen throughout our lives on this earth which will tempt us, test us, pressure and stretch us just like Jesus experienced while here on earth. The bible says the thief (Satan) comes to steal, kill and destroy. Alternately, Jesus said He came that we might have life (God's life in us) and have it more abundantly. The Heavenly Father and Jesus Christ desires all of us to live an abundant life, not only with spiritual and physical prosperity, but also with a joyful, peaceful, unworried, and purposeful life having the fruits of the Holy Spirit in us. This is so much better than a hopeless, helpless, sin-filled life that is doomed to end up in hell for eternity. Men were never intended to go to hell. Hell was not created for man. Mankind was created to live on this earth and have a close fellowship with God.

Now, since Satan was defeated by Jesus, he knows his time and his kingdom on earth are coming to an end. Mortal man and this earth as we know it are also coming to an end. Satan has read the book of Revelation and knows his own demise. So, he is on a rampage in the earth to continue deceiving and destroying whatever he can before the end occurs. We can have an abundant life of God through our Lord Jesus and his Holy Spirit in us. It becomes a matter of how we choose to live our lives. There really is no middle ground. We are now living in the great harvest time Jesus spoke about in the Gospels. Now is the time of gathering people into God's kingdom. There is a separation occurring, yet there are more men, women and children that may yet be physically born and receive Christ. God is patient and will wait for those that are yet to come. But know this, there is coming a time when time is up, then God will announce "It is time for Jesus to return!"

His word says that it is God's desire (His will) for all men and women come to repentance (or to change their lives) and be saved. The same could have been said of the Pharaoh of Egypt. But, if we are honest with ourselves, will all men and women be saved? We all know the answer is no. There will be men and women who will continue to reject God. There will even be believers who haven't taken their salvation relationship with Christ serious enough. They will not attain salvation from God because they still loved the things and sinful pleasures in this world more than their love for God. I can honestly say that from experience that sin is very tempting and can be pleasurable, but only for a limited time. I know because I used to live on the fence and in sin. I now know what and who I am. I was born into sin, lived the life of a sinner, heard the Word of truth - the gospel good news of my salvation in Christ, became born-again into this new life that flows from God the Father that was according to His will, His plan and purpose. The free gift He offers to all, I chose to receive for myself. I encourage you to do the same, to make the same choice. I no longer desire to continue living in sin after becoming a child of God. My heart desire is to please Him and to live my life where I'm not breaking His heart in willful disobedience. He's given the gift of His Spirit and His word to lift me up above the muck and mire of this world.

With that written, a portion of the original question regarding the foundation of "what" and "who" in life has been answered in these two chapters. By all means, it's not all encompassing, but it's only a foundational connection of the spiritual things in life intertwined with an understanding of a number of the physical things, including history, providing a biblical worldview perspective to enable a person to minimize their double mindedness. It's my hope that this will help you in your life-long pursuit of growing in your faith and knowledge of Christ's love as you seek the kingdom of God and His righteousness. Let's move onto the next question of "why."

Chapter 3 – (The "Why" in life)

In chapter 1, it was noted that after Adam and Eve had sinned, their physical and spiritual being changed immediately, they became limited to live by their natural five physical senses and limited in their thoughts, became like the animals around them. They were initially created by God in a higher state of being before sin. All we have to do is observe our own state of being after the fall to recognize this truth. Again, as a young man the majority of what I learned related to this natural-minded physical world and how this natural system worked. On the other hand, my early experience in church greatly lacked any knowledge in regard to how the spiritual was interconnected with this physical world.

The problem was with me. Concisely, it was about not knowing who I was in Christ, also not understanding how to grasp hold of living by faith, nor how to effectively communicate man's spiritual condition with people who were highly educated in the natural things of this life. Those who simply reject anything spiritual and others who would only accept physical scientific answers and evidence to any of the questions posed about whether there was a God. I was unable to interconnect God with the life we live in the here and now in this modern world. Sure, I could've called them all out as sinners and made the claim "I'm saved!" with a smile, just like most believers do in their evangelism efforts. But I could barely tell people what I was saved from, nor did I know anything of value. I was truly an illiterate Christian convert and was not equipped to convert others, let alone disciple others.

Allow me to be a little more open and honest here, it's not like I spent hours and hours, week after week researching and demanding these answers. Like most laymen in church, I had depended on the pastors and leaders to know it all and to bring the required one-hour message each Sunday. Weekdays were mine and I really was only interested in what I wanted to do in my life. All the while in the back of my mind, there were those nagging questions inside of "what, who, why and how."

Many times, in life, good Christian people will just randomly proclaim, "God is in control!" One normally doesn't really think much of it at the time when its spoken, but looking deeper into it, this is usually after something seriously bad has happened in life, or some sudden loss of a home, business, employment, a loved one or the death of a friend. Then a moment later, not all, but some of the same people are reacting to circumstances in life, claiming to find a devil under every rock, or claiming an attack from Satan, expressing a constant need for deliverance. When I heard these things in my youth and as a young man, I'd also remember all of the bad news from the nightly TV news shows. Needless to say, confusion, doubt and unbelief were created and built up within me. It didn't appear God was controlling much of anything and He was allowing things to happen. Thus, there was always this question of "why." Some leaders in the church say the Bible and the gospel are not hard to understand. On the contrary, a person like me, and I'm sure for many others as well, it's not as easy as some may think. Questions in life come to us - why do bad things happen to good people? Or, to bad people? I'll include myself and loved ones in this question as well. Things that are good and bad happen to Christians too. Why do many experience terrible things on this earth? Unfortunately, many don't want the real answer to these questions. That is because many believe God is in complete and total control of everything good and bad on this earth and their lives.

Unfortunately, many will proclaim they are like poor old Job when bad things occur. They refuse to hear that they may have played a part or had some responsibility in each situation whether it was a spiritual or physical situation. In my opinion, the best place to start on this subject of "why" is discovered in the Old Testament book of Job. We touched on Job earlier and I indicated we would revisit and investigate this further.

Most scholars will agree this book is probably one of the oldest books in the Bible, more than likely written before Moses wrote the first five books of what we now call the Old Testament. This book records probably a period of nine months to a year. In roughly 40 chapters of arguing, Job and his so-called friends are going back and forth, we discover through these chapters that Job progressively reveals his own self-righteous attitude, and this question arises within the reader, "why?"

First, lets recognize that Job may not have known about Satan, nor if he even knew Satan existed. Given the text, we can read the explanation of why and how it happened and that it was Satan who did all of the destruction, killed all of Job's children and destroyed his entire livelihood. Job apparently didn't know it was Satan at all. When Satan approached God, he thought God had placed a hedge of protection around Job to where he could not get to him. Satan must not have been paying attention. This proves that our enemy is not omnipotent and omnipresent in this world. Satan wonders around the earth going to and fro, he is not omnipresent. But as is the nature of God He saw what was in Satan's heart, the intended destruction of Job. God couldn't and wouldn't lie to Satan in their conversation. In fact, God is not a liar. God's character and integrity compels Him to be always truthful. Jesus revealed Satan to be a liar and the father of it. God responds to Satan - "look, Job is in your power."

The following will help explain what brought down Job's protection and blessing from God. There are three (3) basic things we know about Job. There's probably more than this, but we are reviewing these to get an understanding of the main question. One item was that Job obviously knew about God. Second item was he knew about blood covenant relationships. And third, he knew about animal sacrifice for the covering of sin. These three items are subjects all to their own and require more time to cover them in detail. We are not delving into the depths of these three subjects at this point, but only the surface of these to grasp the overall picture of what's happening with Job.

It might be safe to say that Job had heard about and took to heart all the stories about God, the Garden of Eden and great, great, great grandpa Adam and grandma Eve as he grew up as a child. We don't know the exact number of generations. There were stories about how God instituted the covenants and animal sacrifices after Adam's fall. The stories were more than likely passed down through the generations of his and other families. He knew about blood covenant agreements. We know covenants of today as basically a written contract, or an agreement between two people, or partnering entities. Blood covenants in Job's day were a common practice with men from the very beginning in Genesis and it's much deeper in relationship in that life and death are associated with keeping or breaking this type of covenant. Today, it continues to be practiced in a few eastern and middle eastern cultures of the world today. Although, today, this practice is performed as a perversion of the original covenant established by God in the beginning. At some point in his life, Job incorporated the practice of animal sacrifices for the covering of sins into his life. We don't know all the details, but there apparently was a point earlier in his life where Job had acted in faith to establish a life-keeping covenant with God and began calling on the name of the Lord in prayer. This covenant was a life-keeping covenant because God tells Satan in the beginning of the book, he could not take Job's life. But we also see this covenant did not include Job's kids or family. Job's covenant was limited.

In regard to how Job knew about God in his life, we get some insight much later in the book where Job repents from his self-righteous attitude and humbles himself when God appears to him out of the whirlwind. Job confesses he had only heard about God before this time with the hearing of the ear, but now he can see God with his eyes and can hear Him with his ears. (paraphrased) Job realizes his error in the presence of God Almighty. Let's recall that repentance is not the same as doing penance. Repenting of sin is not a bad thing. It is actually a good thing needed for the cleansing of our souls from sin. The word repent simply means to change our mind and our direction from sin toward God. Choosing the direction to seek and pursue His righteousness.

Here's the main point in Job's situation. In Chapter 3 verses 25 and 26, it says that Job realized "the thing he greatly feared had come upon him and what he dreaded had happened to him." In chapter 1, we can read that part of his fear and dread is revealed when He was continually offering sacrifices for his children's sin, just in case they were sinning against God. In Chapter 30 verse 15, another part reveals his terrors were turned upon him. This should be a real eye-opener for all believers. Fear and worry. Two main areas that even our Lord Jesus warned us about. Jesus said to avoid these, but to have faith in God (John 14:1) and to take heed or to what we allow ourselves to see, what we allow ourselves to hear and what we allow into our heart and our life. Allowing uncontrolled thoughts of fear and worry will rob us of the fruits of the Spirit. Back to the main question, the one that was raised by Job in this entire book and has been a question in the mind of every man on earth since the fall of Adam, "why did this happen to me?" In Job's case, he was seeking a self-righteous response to justify himself before God. Likewise, in general, every man and woman has asked the question - 'why?'

After Job completes his self-righteous rant, God decides He's had enough of this back and forth among Job's friends. He shows up on the scene, at first speaking by the Holy Spirit through Elihu, then He directly reveals Himself in a whirlwind and God begins to question him. In forty chapters, over the duration of nine months, we read all the accusations, arguments and the complaints of Job and his so-called friends. We should notice immediately from the beginning that Job doesn't call out to God for deliverance in prayer. He just sits there in pain and agony, expressing his self-pity and grief. His friends may have intended to bring him comfort at the start, but eventually they become part of his problem. And, with an accusing wife like the one he had, he wouldn't need an enemy. When God shows up, He leads Job in a line of questioning that leaves Job speechless. Then Job repents and look at what God does here. He doesn't leave Job in this sorry situation. After Job prays for his friends, God totally restores him. Job is completely healed, and God delivers him from Satan's destruction. God provides him with twice as much material goods and children as he had before. Job lives to a good old age, rich and was blessed to see his children's children.

In all that is said and written in this book, God doesn't tell him the answer to the question of "why." I believe this has to do with Job not praying and petitioning God in the very beginning of his ordeal. He began in "self-pity", he argued and complained in his own "self-righteousness." Whenever the word "self- "is involved, this is really a self-centered selfish attitude that should be avoided. Believers are warned against having this attitude.

The question of "why" in this book goes unanswered. So, why didn't God just outright answer this question? He could have, but since this question was not petitioned in prayer, God is not necessarily obligated to provide a response. For most issues in our life, the real question is not necessarily "why." People might think that it is, but it is not. Why is not the real question. The real questions are, "What do I do, when I don't know why?" "Why wasn't the Lord able to protect us, or our loved ones, every day or every week?" "What should I have done or corrected in my life?" We have a responsibility here on earth.

Let this be clear, Job was not under a test in this situation, his own sin removed God's hand and hedge of protection which in turn allowed Satan to destroy his livelihood and family. In regard to the issue of tests and trials, God is not the one who is being tested or tried here on earth to see if He is going to pass or fail a test, we are! For God's obedient children, tests and trials in life are all about whether we are going to have faith and increase in faith or fall back into fear and doubt. Those children who have chosen to be stubborn and disobedient will suffer the consequences of their choices and actions. The sons of disobedience under the sway of the devil and this world will also eventually suffer in their life one way or another. Whether we as children of God (faithful believers) will be true and trust Him and honor our part in this covenant with Christ, or whether we are going to backslide and accuse Him using the question of "why." The goodness of God is also found in His correction and discipline that comes from His word. Tests and trials mainly come through standing up and proclaiming the gospel to a world that may not want to hear it, thus we will receive varying degrees of persecution from unbelievers.

Many theologians, denominations, pastors and believers have wrongly accepted man's doctrine of human reasoning that everything that happens in this earth is under God's complete control and that it is His will to allow bad or evil things in our life. Not true. Job was the one who allowed this into his life, he owned up to it and admitted his own fear and dread. The Bible says that anything that is not of faith, is sin. So, Job knew what his sin was when he attempted to cover for his sin and his children's sin. As some children reach the age of accountability, it's time to accept their own responsibility of repentance from sin and call upon the Lord for help. Job was not offering sacrifices in faith and apparently his children were not honoring God in their lives.

The thing about it is, we are not all-knowing and know the thoughts and intentions within another person's heart and mind. What they've done in the open or what they've done in secret. We really wouldn't know much about a person, unless we actually lived with them. There's only one who can see the intentions of our heart, He is God Almighty. He knows the truth in every situation in life. There will be many things that will happen in this life that we will not fully comprehend or understand. No matter how mature we think we are in the Lord. Even extremely painful situations.

Temptations will continue to come to us during these hard times to turn to God and to shout out - "why!?!?" Realize there is a spiritual danger in this. This question is actually accusing God of the action or circumstance that was performed against us, or maybe even one of our loved ones. The enemy of our lives is called the Accuser of the brethren in the Bible. Let's not act or speak like him. This is why we need mind renewal in spiritual things. Remember when Jesus said that His words are spirit and they are life. Also, remember the Proverb that says the power of life and death are in the tongue. Every word we choose to speak, they are from our spirit. Another scripture Jesus said, 'out of the abundance of the heart the mouth speaks'. We can read in letter of Jude where even Michael the Archangel didn't dare to say anything "accusingly" while contending with the devil over the body of Moses, but only said "the Lord rebuke you." Let us not accuse God of the evil that happens in this world. Satan is called the god of this world. He still has control and dominion here given to him by Adam through the sons of disobedience. As a born-again Spirit-filled Christian, the difference in this age is that Satan is no longer god over the believer. God is good and He is not evil. He is light and in Him there is no darkness (none) at all. The life and ministry of our Lord Jesus while on earth has given us a marvelous example of all the goodness and the love of the Father expressed in Him walking on the earth. He gave us the perfect example of how a man baptized in water and with the Holy Spirit can overcome this world and live in victory over sin and with power with authority in resisting the devil.

Another point to be made regarding the twisting of scripture by only looking at the affairs of this life from the natural perspective, in lieu of from the spiritual. God does not use death, disease, accidents, pain, injury or the like, in order to teach lessons, nor test us. A good and loving God allows what we choose to allow in our life. God is in control in heaven. He is not necessarily in control of this world; Satan is presently and temporarily the god here over the sons of disobedience.

But, if a person becomes a believer, God's kingdom expands in this earth through the heart of that individual. If the person awakes to righteousness, the spiritual kingdom becomes established in their heart. It is true that while living here on earth, Christians will experience trials and tribulations, but these will be from our enemy through the hands and actions of other men, or by our own poor choices in life. The curse of sickness and disease are a result from sin in this world. Accidents and hardships happen because we live and work in a fallen world.

God allows bad and evil things all over this planet to happen. Let's be clear, when these things happen to us, they are absolutely not His will, nor are they His desire. God's creation began with perfection and was intended to be continued throughout the generations. It was not created to be as it is now. That goes for all the murders, rapes, tyranny and evil occurring all over this world. He has had to pass over the sins of mankind since the time after Noah's flood because He created and allowed men to have choice and free-will. Like Cain in the beginning, men of this world have chosen their own rebellious way with the influence of Satan's nature in them.

When God gives His word, He doesn't take it back nor back away from it. When God speaks and gives His word, He speaks from an absolute heart of truth, integrity and holiness that establishes spiritual law which cannot be broken. God doesn't contradict Himself. God's allowance of all the circumstances in life doesn't translate to mean everything that occurs in life reveals His will. An example of this is found in Lamentations 2:31-33. (v33) in the NIV and NKJV. During this time, God had judged Israel's sin and their abominations, to where they were taken into captivity, He had to. He had to punish Israel because they broke the covenant and were not repenting of their sin. But it was not His will to punish them. His will was for them to walk in obedience to the covenant and to be blessed and protected.

When the disciples asked Jesus how to pray, He instructed them and said – "Our Father in heaven, hallowed be your name, Your kingdom come, Your will be done, On earth as it is in heaven...." (Matthew 6:9-10) Why would Jesus teach His disciples to pray this way and to ask for God's will to be done on earth as it is in heaven? Because though His will is being done in heaven, it is not being done on the earth.

Now, here's another problem of some theologians, pastors and many believers who are misrepresenting God and scripture. Usually, a portion of Romans 8:28 is referenced, quoting that He "works all things together for good" when bad things or an unfortunate death occurs. This portion of scripture is taken out of context and incorrectly applied to give an explanation as to why bad things happen in life. When the entire scripture and chapter are read in their context, this portion is in reference to the believer's prayer life. Chapter 8 reveals freedom from the dominion of sin for those who are in Christ, who do not walk according to their flesh, but according to the Spirit. In addition, believers receive sonship through the Spirit, then continues on to how we are to look forward in hope for the redemption of our physical body and ends with a comment on "if God is for us, who can be against us?" Then answers the question - that nothing will separate us from His love.

Let's back up a couple verses and read this more carefully -

Romans 8:26-28 (NKJV) – "Likewise the Spirit also helps in our weaknesses. For we do not know what we should pray for as we ought, but the Spirit Himself makes intercession for us with groanings which cannot be uttered. Now He who searches the hearts knows what the mind of the Spirit is, because He makes intercession for the saints according to the will of God. And we know that all things work together for good to those who love God, to those who are called according to His purpose."

Just reading these few verses in context, the subject is about believers praying in the Spirit. It's not about bad and evil events happening to us and others around us, nor is it about the trials of life. It's most definitely not about good things coming from the death of a loved one. It's about prayer to God with groanings in the Spirit. As believers pray in the Spirit, God knows their heart and knows the mind of the Spirit because He is One (in unity) with the Father and the Son. And, while in prayer, Jesus instructs us to pray having faith in God. Mountain moving faith. Faith as a mustard seed. Faith to believe we receive answers to our prayers as we ask in accordance with His will. And as in many times during prayer, there are times of not having the right words to express in our understanding, where when if we allow Him to give us the utterance, He will assist us in our intercessory prayer in the language of angels and the various tongues of men.

Now, "to those who love God" was underscored for a reason. This portion of the scripture is linked with "things working together for good." We have to ask a few questions, "What is this type of love for God? Is it based upon our emotional feelings of love? Are there people in the world today who claim to love God, but don't have a clue as to who He really is?" Well, it's not based in the emotional realm and it's not just an acknowledgement. The gospel of John reveals the true love for God in Chapter 14 verses 19-21, 23 and 24:

John 14:19-21, 23, 24 (NKJV) – Jesus instructing His disciples, "A little while longer and the world will see Me no more, but you will see Me. Because I live, you will live also. At that day you will know that I am in My Father, and you in Me, and I in you. He who has my commandments and keeps them, it is he who loves Me. And he who loves Me will be loved by My Father, and I will love him and manifest (reveal) Myself to him...If anyone loves Me, he will keep My word; and

My Father will love him, and We will come to him and make our home with him. He who does not love Me does not keep My words, and the word which you hear is not Mine but the Father's who sent Me."

Love is equated with keeping (observing and doing) His commandments, doing His word which comes from the Father. In John's gospel, Jesus commanded His disciples to love one another. Love is not just a feeling or having an emotional condition. When we love someone, we do things for them. We respect, honor, and value them, and are even submissive to them. This is true love for God and it is the fulfillment of the law. Since God is love and His love has been shed abroad in our hearts by the Spirit, the Apostle Paul reveals what love truly is and how it is intended to be expressed in our life –

> 1 Corinthians 13: 4-8 (AMPC) – "Love endures with patience and serenity, love is kind and thoughtful, and is not jealous or envious; love does not brag and is not proud or arrogant. It is not rude; it is not self-seeking; it is not provoked (nor overly sensitive and easily angered); it does not take into account a wrong endured. It does not rejoice at injustice, but rejoices with the truth (when right and truth prevail). Love bears all things (regardless of what comes), believes all things (looking for the best in each one), hopes all things (remaining steadfast during difficult times), endures all things (without weakening. Love never fails (it never fades nor ends)."

Let's ask another question, "Are all believers loving one another as Christ commanded us?" Hmm, a difficult question we probably shouldn't answer. There are denominational and non-denominational cliques in each and every church that do love one another, but not everyone in the body of Christ are loving each other as the Lord instructed. "Are there people attending church who may not be fully committed to the Lord and His will in their lives?" Unfortunately, there are. Love for Jesus and our Father relates directly to our passion for and commitment to His commandments and His word. This is how the Father manifests himself and makes His home with us and Jesus in us. Now, if God is for us and living with each of us, what can man do to us? In 1John 4:8 the Apostle John states that God is Love. So, in 1 Corinthians 13 Paul's revelation of this love describes the nature of our Father God with His children. And as believers, we are instructed to follow Him and walk in this kind of love.

We are not finished with this subject of "why." In 2nd Corinthians 11, let's review the sufferings that the Apostle Paul experienced as a believer, (vs 23-28)

> "...in labors more abundant, in stripes above measure, in prisons more frequently, in deaths often. From the Jews five times I received forty stripes minus one. Three times I was beaten with rods; once I was stoned; three times I was shipwrecked; a night and a day I was in the deep; in journeys often, in perils of waters, in perils of robbers, in perils of my own countrymen, in perils of the Gentiles, in perils in the city, in perils in the wilderness, in perils in the sea, in perils among false brethren; in weariness and toil, in sleeplessness often, in hunger and thirst, in fastings often, in cold and nakedness – besides the other things, what comes upon me daily; my deep concern for all the churches..." (NKJV)

If we read about Paul's conversion on the road to Damascus, Jesus tells Ananias that Paul will suffer for His name sake. Then later in the book of Acts (26:16-18), as Paul recites his testimony before King Agrippa, (Paul reciting what Jesus told him) –

> "... for I have appeared to you for this purpose, to make you a minister and a witness both of the things which you have seen and of the things which I will yet reveal to you. I

will deliver you from the Jewish people, as well as from the Gentiles, to whom I will now send you, to open their eyes, in order to turn them from darkness to light, and from the power of Satan to God, that they may receive forgiveness of sins and an inheritance among those who are sanctified by faith in Me..." (NKJV)

The type of deliverance Jesus is referring to is regard to the persecutions from both the Jews and the Gentiles. And as Paul noted earlier in all of his sufferings, he was also delivered from all of those he listed. Yet, in all of Paul's list of sufferings, it's interesting to notice that sickness and disease are not mentioned as part of his suffering. The stoning he received from persecution ended up with him being brought back to life and physically healed. Though the devil tried to destroy him many times through the hands of men, the Lord divinely delivers and restores him each time. If we are willing to believe it, divine healing works. Being raised from the dead is as possible today as it was then. Even though in Christ there is a suffering we are to endure from persecution, He keeps us and heals us and delivers us from the snares of the enemy.

Paul confirms the list of suffering through persecution noted in the following -

Colossians 1:23-25 (NKJV) –

"...if indeed you continue in the faith, grounded and steadfast, and are not moved away from the hope of the gospel which you heard, which was preached to every creature under heaven, of which I, Paul, became a minister. I now rejoice in my sufferings for you, and fill up in my flesh what is lacking in the afflictions of Christ, for the sake of His body, which is the church, of which I became a minister according to the stewardship from God which was given to me for you, to fulfill the word of God..."

Here's one more example of "why" in the New Testament. In Luke 13: 1-5, Jesus and His disciples were walking, and the subject came up in discussion from the news they heard of what Pilate had done in killing some Galileans by mingling their blood with the animal sacrifices. And they talked about how the Tower of Siloam had suddenly fallen, killing quite a number of people. What did Jesus say in response to them? He said "...but unless you repent, you will all likewise perish..." This seems like an unusual response to their discussion. What was Jesus saying here? The disciples were asking the wrong question of "why." Even though we know it's God will and desire for all men to come to repentance and be saved, other questions arise – Will all men choose to be saved? We know the answer is no. Will someone die tonight not knowing the Lord? We know the answer is yes. From this we can understand that there were also people living when Jesus walked on earth who perished without knowing God. Jesus was saying that the important thing to keep in mind at all times is that we should live our lives in a lifestyle of repentance all the days of our life. That means changing our direction from error to correction into God's will be based upon His word and in being led by the Holy Spirit. Because we don't know exactly what's going to happen from day to day. And, nor are we aware of, nor responsible for how other people will choose to live their lives. We are each individually responsible for our own life, how we live each day and how we speak.

Allow further perspective, when unbelievers are under the influence of deceptions from our enemy, as sons of disobedience, their sins are under the judgement of God and His wrath is against them. Remember, the wages of sin is death. Sons of disobedience in this world are living their lives in ignorance of God with blindness from the enemy of their souls. This is all due to their own sin and rebellion. Then, when a man chooses to accept Jesus as their Lord and Savior, believe He was raised from the dead, becoming born-again by the imperishable word of God, this person is translated from the kingdom of darkness and comes under the influence and direction of the Lord. But this person still gets to keep their free-will. God wants us to love him of our own free-will and choosing, through faith in Him. He doesn't try to control us to change us into programed robots. He desires us to know Him individually on a personal level, know His ways and know His goodness. He has given us His book to know and grow in Christ, understand and know we need to put away sin and learn to walk in His ways of grace and in right standing with Him as a new creation. To be led of the Holy Spirit and His word.

In the man-made doctrine of God controlling everything on earth, people are drawn to it and like it because it appeals to their emotions and human reasoning, and their rationality of placing all responsibility on God. It is an attempt to reason everything in their heads regarding the events happening in the world with the destruction and problems around them. This doctrine greatly reduces their reliance on having any faith in God and explains away bad and evil things that happen. What this really does it places the blame on God and accuses Him of doing evil. This doctrine contradicts Proverbs 3: 5-8. Human reliance on their own reasoning and rationalization to explain things in life is completely and thoroughly wrong and dangerous.

Now, as noted earlier, God is in complete control somewhere, and that is in heaven. There will come a time where His will and His prophetic word will be fulfilled in this earth. His word will not return to Him void but accomplish the task for which it is sent. When this age is over, and we are taken to be with our Lord, He will be our Lord. No more fight over the American Constitution, no more fight for the republic or so-called democracy and no more voting rights. No more tyranny from mankind nor influences from the enemy of our soul. Jesus will take His place as King of kings and Lord of lords. We will take our place as a royal priesthood unto God, understanding our inheritance with Christ. It will be a kingdom, and not a republic, nor a democracy. But it will be a good and honorable kingdom full of God's grace. There will not be any evil there. No sickness, no disease, no curse and no more pain or tears. God Himself will wipe away all our tears. We will be in His presence, in fullness of joy and peace. We will be released from our old bodies of dead sinful flesh and into the hope of our glory, our new bodies.

Some may ask the question, "What will help our unsaved loved ones?" Pray and ask for God's grace (favor) and mercy (love) upon them. Ask the Father to give them more time and to send perfect laborers (believers) of Christ across their path with the right message. Take authority over the enemy trying to blind their eyes and heart. Pray they will have ears to hear and eyes to understand the truth of Father God and discern the lies from the enemy. Stand in faith and believe they will receive truth in their heart and invite Jesus to be Lord in their lives. The promise is that God desires all men (and women) to be saved. We need to allow someone to plant the word, another to water the word and for God to bring the increase from the harvest of souls.

Chapter 4 – How - (How to Live this Life on Earth)

Hopefully, the first, second and third chapters of what, who and why will be of some help to you. It is not a comprehensive perspective, but are what I would call the essentials needed in our Christian way of life. Remember this is only a brief guide. It's not an all-encompassing 10 step plan to instant wealth and health, nor a tried-and-true formula for instant success and comfort in life. Getting into the subject of "how" presents many challenges for most Christians. It's unfortunate, but many only want to keep Him at a distance only as their Savior for future fire insurance. Most of these will usually say that He is Lord out of one side of their mouth, but in reality, they live their lives without His input or involvement as Lord. What they are really implying is they still have a lust for the things offered in this world. John identified this lust as the pride of life, the lust of the eyes and lust of the flesh. But, if you are part of the other group that has chosen the path of a life-long pursuit of truly knowing Him, then don't allow negative thoughts and the circumstances from this world to distract you from the pursuit of knowing Him who bought you with the price of the precious blood of Christ. You are not alone, there are many of us out here in the same pursuit. And, our Helper, the Holy Spirit is here with us and is in us to guide us into truth.

Keep in mind, as long as we are living in our flesh and in the confines of this world system of sin, curse and unbelief, there will be serious challenges to what we believe with tests, trials and sadly tragedy for many. Jesus Himself said as much in explaining the meaning of the Parable of the Sower. And in this life as a Christian, it will appear to us that there is more resistance from this world than there are those who are for us. This is a world that will resist you and this comes directly from the enemy of our souls, the devil. We need to be aware and learn of His devices and methods, in order to know how to win in this struggle on earth. Jesus our Lord, our example, He overcame this world and told His disciples to take heart because through faith in Him it is now possible to live in victory and battle the enemy. Paul describes it as the fight of faith. In addition, we are given the promise of the Spirit by the in-filling and baptism of the Holy Spirit and knowledge in the Word of God, believers can overcome sin and this world in the same manner Jesus overcame.

In this chapter, several spiritual and scriptural "helps" will be presented that every Christian should purpose to develop in the renewal of their mind. But in order to develop this there are several subjects to be introduced for the whole concept of "how" comes together:

Faith/Fear/Awe/Reverence
Doubt and Unbelief
The Blood Covenant
The Believer's Authority
Prayer/Conscience

The foundation of faith and walking in this life by faith are two critical elements in which every believer in Christ should grow and be grounded in on a consistent basis.

Faith is the foundation and bedrock of Christian living. Faith is needed for all believers to understand and grasp the spiritual truth and the reality of our new birth in Christ. All this is in addition to understanding all the good things of what our Father God has provided believers through our Lord Jesus Christ. In other words, every believer should come to a recognition of what can be described as an "overall big picture" Christian based worldview of how God originally designed us in the beginning with Adam and Eve, the fall of mankind, our redemption and release from the dominion of sin, starting from the beginning in Genesis to the end of Revelation.

> W.E. Vine Expository Dictionary defines biblical faith – "primarily, 'firm persuasion', a conviction based upon hearing, is used in the NT always of 'faith in God or Christ, or things spiritual."

It's unfortunate, those that are taught the subject of living by faith are in the minority in the body of Christ. As a seasoned Christian, I've become familiar with the various teachings available on faith, but it wasn't until recent years in my life that the Holy Spirit has led me into a deeper understanding of what the walk of faith is about. It's much more than just having a doctrinal belief system or an acknowledgement that God exists in heaven somewhere. Let's review the four following scriptures:

Romans 10: 17 (NKJV) "...So then faith comes by hearing, and hearing by the word of God."

Hebrews 11: 1 & 6 (NKJV) "Now faith is the substance of things hoped for, the evidence of things not seen,"..."But without faith it is impossible to please him, for he who comes to God must believe that He is, and He is a rewarder to those who diligently seek Him."

Hebrews 4: 12 & 13 (NKJV) "For the word of God is living and powerful, and sharper than any two-edged sword, piercing even to the division of soul and spirit, and of joints and marrow, and is a discerner of the thoughts and intents of the heart."

The Holy Spirit teaches us in Hebrews chapter 11 three essential truths about faith. First, it defines what faith is in the first verse. Faith is always in the now, the present, not in the past nor sometime in the future. Faith means to be fully persuaded or convinced every moment of every day that God and His word are truth, the final word in our life. All the promises of God are yes and amen in Christ. Faith has substance and is tangible in the spirit realm of heaven. Faith provides a God-like hope of expectation for overcoming in this life. Our faith is the evidence of what is not seen because we have chosen to believe, to fully trust in Him beyond what this world may throw at us.

Secondly, Hebrews 11 teaches faith in Him always pleases our heavenly Father. If we desire to please Him in our life, we need to understand and do His will. This requires learning His ways and His thoughts. We should also recognize this faith in Him will require a consecration, a separation from the world system of living for themselves and self-centeredness. The word says, "Be holy, for I am holy." (1Peter 1: 16 NKJV) This will require consistent work on our part. The type of work that requires renewing our mind and giving our full attention to the study of His word.

Thirdly, Hebrews teaches that God responds to those who diligently seek Him and walk this life of faith in Him, our Father openly rewards us in this physical realm. Romans 10:17 gives further instruction on how believers are to receive and grow in this faith, that is, through "hearing" God's word. To apply this in our life, we must actually speak the word of God aloud from our mouths, to hear with our ears the truth of God's word. By doing this, faith will rise in our heart, once faith and trust have come, then we must begin to put this faith into action based upon what we have heard. Not just once in a while, but on a continual and consistent basis. Spending quality time, daily reading/study, speaking and hearing His word, consistently and diligently. As this is done, this will contribute to the process of learning and renewing our mind. Faith works by changing how we think or what we give thought to, and in how we believe. The transformation of our old nature into His image and nature occurs by hearing the imperishable word of God. Over the process of time, we grow in Christ and obtain His wisdom, His integrity, His character, His honor, His spiritual understanding and knowledge. Through His word and with the help of the Holy Spirit, we become grounded in Him. As we are diligent in seeking God's kingdom in our lives, He will reveal Himself to us. Our old ways of thinking become changed to think like Him. He's not making us into robots, but we need to come up to His level and learn His ways. As we grow and exercise our faith and trust in Him, we can trust Him for those things we ask for in accordance with His will. We trust and believe we have them.

The following few bullet points and statements are copied from a healing equip class I taught recently at my local church, with a few notes added -

We should not allow our faith to be wishy-washy, doubtful or pretentious. 1Timothy 1: 5 talks about having a sincere faith. If we know it's possible to have a sincere faith, it must also be possible to have a pretentious faith.

James 1: 6 – "...but let him ask in faith, with no doubting, for he who doubts is like a wave of the sea driven and tossed by the wind. For let not that man suppose that he will receive anything from the Lord, for he is a double-minded man, unstable in all his ways." (NKJV)

Our faith in God the Father and His will regarding healing should be without question.

John 17: 17 – Jesus stated God's word is truth.

John 14: 6 – Jesus also stated "I am the way, the truth and the life. No one comes to the Father except through Me." (NKJV)

Acts 10:38 – "...how God anointed Jesus of Nazareth with the Holy Spirit and with power, who went about doing good and healing ALL who were oppressed by the devil, for God was with Him." (NKJV) [ALL means ALL, it doesn't mean some or some of the time, it means ALL and it must be His will ALL the time!]

Mark 11:22–25, Jesus stated to have "faith in God". Also told us to speak to our mountains.

Eph. 2: 8 – understand our faith is a precious gift from God. It is valued by God. Don't treat it lightly.

Heb. 11: 1 – Faith defined, is "the substance of things hoped for and the evidence of things not seen." (NKJV)

Heb. 11: 3 – by faith we understand our creation.
Heb. 11: 6 – our faith pleases God the Father.

2Cor. 4: 13 – we have been given the same Spirit of faith, we believe therefore we speak.

2Cor. 5: 7 – For we walk by faith, not by sight. (NKJV)
Hab. 2: 4 - ...but the just shall live by faith. (NKJV)
Heb. 10:38 – " " " " " " "
Rom. 1: 17 - " " " " " " "
Gal. 3: 11 - " " " " " " " "

These are a few of the scriptures that address the faith of the believer and truth of God's word. As mentioned earlier, there are many different levels of faith and understanding among all believers. From a pretentious faith to a real fully persuaded faith. Faith has substance and is tangible with Father God. Though the evidence of it is dealing with the unseen, faith is more real than this natural physical existence. Its more real than our circumstances and our own emotional feelings. Faith is more real than what can be –

seen with the human eye.

touched with our hands.

heard with our ears.

sensed by taste with our mouth and tongue.

or by our sense of smell in our nose.

Faith is believing the "unseen" realm is more real to us than our own physical realm. We are more spirit than we know or realize.

A promise in 1Samuel 2:30 (NKJV) – God says, "...for those who honor Me I will honor, and those who despise Me shall be lightly esteemed." We honor God when we choose to value Him and take Him at His word. He holds and values His own word above Himself.

Warning - it's when we become complacent and treat His word either in a lackadaisical attitude or treat it in a careless manner as if it had no value and means truly little to us, that's when we are inviting trouble into our home by letting our guard down. Doing this means we are not esteeming or valuing Him. It's despising Him. On the other hand, it is an honor to God when we value His word as a precious gift meant for our good and well-being. The Father takes pleasure in rewarding our faith. There is a Psalm that agrees with this that says He is pleased when His people prosper. In Joshua 1: 8-9, in paraphrase it says as we meditate on His word day and night and observe to do it, we will prosper and have great success.

> Mark 11:23-24 (NKJV), Jesus said, "Have faith in God. For assuredly, I say to you, whoever says to this mountain, 'Be removed and be cast into the sea,' and does not doubt in his heart, but believes that those things he says will be done, he will have whatever he says. Therefore I say to you, whatever things you ask when you pray, believe that you receive them, and you will have them."

We see here the basic principle inherent in the Godkind of faith: believing with the heart and saying it with the mouth. Jesus believed Father God's word, and He spoke things into being. God the Father believed it, and He also spoke things into being.

> 2 Corinthians 4: 13 (NKJV), Paul speaking of having faith quoting Psalm 116:10, "And since we have the same spirit of faith, according to what is written, I believed and therefore I spoke, we also believe and therefore speak, ..."

A mis-guided preacher posted a statement on Facebook a number of years ago having commented on God's sovereignty and how God had no need to have faith for Himself because He is God Almighty, the all-powerful and omnipotent One. In his mind and through human reasoning he was led to believe wrongly about God and His nature. If God didn't have faith at all, then none of us would even exist nor live here on earth. This is ridiculous to our thinking! Jesus operated on this earth in faith. He willingly went to the cross, faced certain death and took our sin upon Himself in faith! His faith was based on God's word of raising Him from the grave and conquering death on our behalf!

We just read the definition of faith in Hebrew 11:1. This verse reveals that God had the substance of our universe and creation in His heart and mind and the evidence of mankind's existence in His heart before they were brought into this physical realm. Verse 3 further confirms our understanding the worlds were framed by the word of God, so that things which are seen were not made of things which are visible. Paul also confirms in Romans 4:17 (NKJV) "... in the presence of Him whom he believed – "God, who gives life to the dead and calls those things which do not exist as though they did;..."

God has faith in you to become an overcomer in this world through Christ! As a believer in Christ, we have the God-given privilege and honor to be imitators of our Lord Jesus and the Heavenly Father by speaking and believing the Word of God that will create and produce results in our lives. God's word is His will for all of us. Faith originates from God who created the universe by this faith, and in the same way Jesus cursed the fig tree to teach His disciples on the subject of faith. This is so awesome and mind-blowing at the same time. This is beyond normal comprehension and reasonable human understanding.

Sadly, most believers in the body of Christ today do not choose to believe that this is available for themselves. Many will say God heals, but also say that healing may not be His will for them. Others will put it off to some future ministry event or say that God is going to do certain things at a certain time in the near future. No, we must believe that faith is always in the moment of now, not to be delayed to some point in the future. Jesus never said to "come back tomorrow, tomorrow is healing day!" or "come back next week, Tuesday at 2pm is healing hour!" No no no! We need mind renewal, in that, our faith only works through the love that God has placed in our heart, Galatians 5: 6. This faith is fully convinced and persuaded God is true to keep His word, and His word is absolute truth, John 17: 17. He watches over His word to perform it, Jeremiah 1:12. His word accomplishes the task for which it is sent, Isaiah 55:11. He sent His word and healed them, Psalm 107: 20. (Paraphrased)

Another step in this faith process. Not only are we to hear and believe God's Word; a believer's walk of faith requires them to be doers of His Word. As paraphrased earlier with Joshua 1: 8 – 9, these scriptures are integral with the following scripture found in James:

James 1: 22 (NKJV)," But be doers of the word, and not hearers only, deceiving yourselves. For if anyone is a hearer of the word and not a doer, he is like a man observing his natural face in a mirror; for he observes himself, goes away, and immediately forgets what kind of man he was. But he who looks into the perfect law of liberty and continues in it, and is not a forgetful hearer but a doer of the work, this one will be blessed in what he does."

In John's gospel, Jesus also defined "being a doer" when He made such statements as, "... that you bear much fruit....", and "...greater works than these shall you do...." The conclusion to the subject of faith is found through our Lord Jesus. We should be always looking to Him who is called the author and finisher of our faith. (Heb.12: 2) Part of how we are to "look" to Him is by studying His Words, study His lifestyle and how He lived as our example put into practice in our life. John instructs us, "... to walk as He walked." On earth, we are commissioned by the Lord to destroy the works of the devil ourselves, overcome the dominion of sin in our life, make known the manifold wisdom of God to the principalities and powers in the heavenly places, walk as Jesus walked, being fully persuaded and confident in faith with God and have love for our fellow brothers and sisters in the body of Christ. Thus, fulfilling the commandment of our Lord.

Believe it or not, that was Faith in a nutshell. Believe me when I say that was not an exhaustive study on the subject, and I guarantee there is more information available beyond this book. Along with faith, believers need a healthy understanding of what the Bible refers to in several places in scripture as 'The fear of the Lord.' And to know the differences among the various types of fear. When I refer to healthy understanding, the intent is to also recognize the fact there has been an unhealthy understanding of fear in the church body that extends from ancient times up to our present modern-day era. Due to the sin-nature that has been passed down to us, the fear we are most familiar with has been a part of our nature from childhood.

> Webster defines the word to mean – FEAR, n.: a coming suddenly upon, fear, danger; 1. A painful emotion or passion excited by the expectation of evil, or the apprehension of impending danger; apprehension; anxiety; solicitude; alarm; dread. 2. (a) Apprehension of incurring, or solicitude to avoid, God's wrath; the trembling and awful reverence felt toward the Supreme Being. (b) Respectful reverence for men of authority or worth. 3. That which causes, or which is the object of, apprehension or alarm; source or occasion of terror; danger; dreadfulness.

> FEAR, v.: to frighten, to be afraid,...1. To feel a painful apprehension of; to be afraid of; to consider or expect with emotion of alarm or solicitude. 2. To have a reverential awe of; to solicitous to avoid the displeasure of. 3. To be anxious or solicitous for. 4. To suspect; to doubt. 5. To affright; to terrify; to drive away or prevent approach of by fear. Syn. — To apprehend; dread; reverence; venerate.

FEAR, v. To be in apprehension of evil; to be afraid; to feel anxiety on account of some expected evil.

The definition above comes from the Webster dictionary in the public domain which is regarded by many as an outdated version of the English language. But I reference it due to the fact that our modern English language has been diluted or eroded to the point of not having the same meanings as in the past. In general, most people today typically think of the terror aspect of fear. In fact, in Webster's definition above, there were many scriptural references that I had removed to minimize the definition length provided as examples of explanation that modern dictionaries no longer reference. I like the Webster definition, in the noun usage there is more definition that appears to really fit the meaning on its surface, it is having profound reverential awe of God.

In my youth and into early adulthood, I recall the fear of God was preached from the pulpit with the negative perspective of the terror of God because in their mind we were all "sinners" committing sin all the time and needed to be in fear of going to hell. I didn't know it at the time, but this is the unhealthy part mentioned earlier. Unfortunately, the world-wide church body has leaders, elders and pastors in positions that should be dismissed from their responsibilities in the church because of their dis-service to the sheep as under-shepherds. Their motivation was and is intended to maintain control over the church body through the terror aspect of fear, along with other aspects that involve manipulation and making sure there's a monthly paycheck for the leader(s). The Lord will eventually uproot them out of the church. Recall the parable of the 'wheat and tares.' Don't take this the wrong way. The word of God says to give to Him, to do it generously and with a cheerful heart. His word challenges us to do this to put Him to the test with our giving. We do this in faith, being fully persuaded He will supply all our need according to Hs riches in glory by Christ

Jesus. Once we give in faith, the leaders and pastors have a tremendous responsibility to be led of the Spirit to faithfully handle the finances for the furtherance of the Gospel and His kingdom.

Regarding fear, we should also be aware that our Lord Jesus did address the issue of fear in Luke 12:4-5 (NKJV) -

> "And I say to you, My friends, do not be afraid of those who kill the body, and after that have no more that they can do. But I will show you whom you should fear: Fear Him who, after He has killed, has power to cast into hell; yes, I say to you, fear Him!"

Admittedly, I'm not an expert when it comes to understanding the Hebrew text from the Old Testament, because of the difficulty of the language, but I do think it would be apropos to interject a brief narrative in order to understand the healthy aspect of this word that is prevalent throughout the Bible and comprehend what Christ stated in the scripture above. There are intricacies associated with translation of Hebrew into the English language because it was a dead language until recently. There are numerous nuances and usage of Hebrew letters and words that are translated into the one English word - 'fear.'

In the Old Testament, fear is used in the book of Exodus with focus on terror. In several other books of the Old Testament, the fear of God is focusing on reverence for Him. In the book of Proverbs, the fear of God is equated with the beginning of wisdom and knowledge. Proverbs includes the instruction of wisdom is to hate evil, and it involves departing from evil. Then the Hebrew, depending on usage, can also translate to 'be afraid; fear not; stand in awe of; reverence and honor. What all of this indicates is that during the Exodus of Israel, God's judgments against Egypt and their gods revealed an aspect of Himself that struck terror into their hearts to let His people go. At Mt. Sinai when His people rebelled and sinned in worship of the golden calf as their new god, Moses and God had to judge and punish them for their sin. A terrible fear came upon all of those who remained afterward. Other occurrences in the Old Testament were specifically written that identified why their fear related to being terrified. God had to pass judgement on their sin, which was due to their disobedience and rebellion. God didn't want to judge them. He sent warning after warning after warning through many of His prophets of what they were doing violated their blood covenant agreement. The people rejected His warnings which brought punishment on themselves. Later in the Bible, we find the other aspects of this fear included words that are more synonymous in relating to having reverence, awe and honor of God.

Just to be clear, the word 'awe' simply means – a strong feeling of fear or respect and also wonder; the word 'reverence' simply means – honor or respect that is felt for or shown to (someone or something), deference; especially: profound adoring awed respect; and the word 'honor' simply means – respect that is given to someone who is admired with high moral standards of behavior. Several synonyms of 'honor' describe it in a much better way, they are – honesty, integrity, righteousness, and uprightness.

Now, we understand the English word fear does involve some level of terror, but it is not the dominant aspect or force when we consider the other words that are synonymous with the word fear. If we review the words of Jesus in Luke 12: 4-5, He is basically stating don't give place to the fear of man and that they may be able to kill this physical body we currently live in, but fear Him who has the power to cast soul and spirit into hell, that is the Father. This is not a threat of terror or of torment in hell from Jesus. It's a revelation of God the Father that His holiness and justice will settle the future fate of many. Yes, God is love, first and foremost. He is good and its His goodness that leads us to repentance. God is also right, fair and just in all of His judgements. He is much more than just being a God of love. He knows every heart and mind. It's unfortunate, but there will be people who reject Him. It's when we have made the choice to believe in Christ and His resurrection to be saved, then later in life we choose to walk completely away from Him breaking relationship. We are acting like Judas who betrayed the Lord. Normal people would judge that we deserve to go to hell for this sin. God would do the same and did it with Judas. If we look at Luke chapter 12 again, but skip down to verses 6-7, Jesus instructs the believers to not fear hell because God values us.

In my Bible, the New King James Version, there are at least thirty-three (33) scripture references that instruct us to live in 'the fear of the Lord.' Since we are living in NT times, let's review Acts 9: 31 (NKJV) -

> "Then the churches throughout Judea, Galilee, and Samaria had peace and were edified. And walking in the fear of the Lord and in the comfort of the Holy Spirit, they were multiplied."

The reading of this verse it would appear contradictory at first glance when we read the words fear and comfort in the same sentence. What's also unusual is that in the previous verse, the churches had peace and were edified. Well, it's not a contradiction. Evidently walking our daily life in the fear of the Lord gives us this peace and comfort that comes from Holy Spirit. The verse is talking about (from W.E. Vine) the reverential side of fear that inspires a constant carefulness in dealing with others in His 'fear.'

Another Hebrew teacher, Chaim Bentorah, I've given time to reading some of his material in recent years has a perspective of this reverential awe of God that communicates an adoration aspect in the following:

> (Bentorah, Hebrew Word Study, revealing the heart of God) – "There is only one thing that can harm God, and that is if we betray our love for Him, if we abuse His love and

break His heart. With this understanding, we do not keep from sin because we fear that God will punish us. We avoid sin because we fear we may wound (or break) God's heart."

Walking life in the fear of the Lord is actually a good thing for us. It is a good fear, not a fear of terror or dread. It is just as important to follow it as Jesus taught us. As we walk and live out our days on earth, the reverence, awe and honor we have for God and the respect for things of God provides blessings of living with peace of mind and in the comfort provided by Holy Spirit.

Our reverence of God should stand alone on its own in our hearts, but it is not to be confused with other types of fears that originates in this world, from the enemy of our soul, from spiritual tormentors which daily bombard our mind with thoughts, and fears that come from others that are considered to be sons of disobedience. As believers, we must remember who we are in Christ and know the weapons of our warfare – God's word, (2Cor.10:4). In the following verse there is a promise.

2Timothy 1: 7 (NKJV), "... For God has not given us a spirit of fear, but of power and of love and of a sound mind."

This verse is stating that God has not given us a spirit of fear (terror to be afraid), but of power (in the Name of Jesus) and of love (God's love has been placed in us) and of a sound mind (for we have the mind of Christ). (2Cor. 2:16).

Doubt and Unbelief. In the modern world we live in today, the level of doubt and unbelief is unparalleled. This includes the many varied denominational persuasions within the worldwide church body as a whole. Much of it has to do with disunity and division that exists, which is contrary to the Bible. We can also certainly find numerous reasons as to why God's blessings don't necessarily always come to pass during a believer's life, but the most frequent cause is simply doubt, unbelief, lifestyle and impatience on the individual's part. Jesus had to deal with unbelief in own His hometown of Nazareth, he could do no mighty works there, found in Matt.13:53-58. Truly, there are no limitations on God's part. He is willing and able to do what He has promised and given. Most of the time, the problem is with us. However, we must choose to exercise our faith (put into practice), the faith freely given to us. Faith is a fruit of the Holy Spirit who lives in us –

Galatians 5: 22 (NKJV)," But the fruit of the Spirit is love, joy, peace,

longsuffering, kindness, goodness, faithfulness, gentleness, self-control."

Faith is a gift from God –

Ephesians 2: 8 (NKJV), "... For by grace you have been saved through faith, and that not of yourselves; it is the gift of God, ..."

Our faith is also linked to our knowledge or what we know and understand in Christ –

2 Peter 1:1-4 (NKJV),"... To those who have obtained like precious faith with us by the righteousness of our God and Savior Jesus Christ: Grace and peace be multiplied to you in the knowledge of God and of Jesus our Lord, as His divine power has given to us all things that pertain to life and godliness, through the knowledge of Him who called us by glory and virtue, ..."

What we think on is how we will be -
Proverbs 23:7 (NKJV), "... For as he (a man) thinks in his heart, so is he."

The problem is not that we don't have faith. The problem occurs when we don't allow our faith to work because we don't keep our minds stayed on God's Word and His promises. Keeping our minds stayed on God's Word will help us release our faith and this thereby reciprocates the release of God's work and His power in our lives.

> James 1: 6 (NKJV) – "...but let him ask in faith, with no doubting, for he who doubts is like a wave of the sea driven and tossed by the wind. For let not that man suppose that he will receive anything from the Lord, for he is a double-minded man, unstable in all his ways."

In order to add substance to this faith, a believer should attain what may be best described as having a New Covenant Mindset along with an understanding of the Believer's Authority. Several years ago, I purchased some cassette tapes from a well-known teaching ministry to listen, learn and grow in Christ. I listened to them many times over several years. They were very insightful for my early Christian growth and they revealed many things that were foundational in my early walk with the Lord. But I need to be totally honest at this point, when my wife and I attempted to apply our God-given authority in prayer, we ended up disappointed and discouraged more times than not. Over time, we became discouraged and were eventually pulled back into doubt and unbelief. In the Word, we found the scriptures that promised our authority and then we wondered why only a few things appeared to work, but many others would not.

As I look back at that time in our life, I understand now how ignorant we really were of the things of God, even though we had great teachers around us. Another moment of honesty, we would get all excited hearing prosperity messages, healing messages, faith messages, etc. But we would also ignore the other messages regarding honesty, honor, integrity, judgement, etc., and the love for this world as described by the Apostle John - the pride of life, the lust of the eyes and lust of the flesh. One could honestly say I had a bad case of the "tickled ear" syndrome. Please don't misunderstand, we were not against God's promise of prosperity, nor against His divine healing for us and His children, nor the faith messages we heard on those tapes. The problem was completely on us. We have since learned our lesson to avoid the tickled ear and have moved on into a deeper walk in God's grace and mercy. All glory, praise and thanks to the Lord.

Many of our English words that are associated or synonymous with the word "authority" are avoided by most people in America, because people that live here do not like to be told what to do. The associated words are obedience, submission and subjection. Although the majority will follow authority to keep their jobs, become law-abiding citizens, or avoid being caught by the law, most people in today's culture believe they are free to do whatever they please, whatever is right in their own eyes. (As it is noted in the last scripture in the book of Judges.)

In the Christian world today, in general, if you were to ask most of them if they have authority in the Name of Jesus, they will look at you with straight faces and say, 'yes I do.' Then if you were to ask them why they have this authority or to provide an explanation, many will probably have a blank look on their face. Some might attempt a guess. It really is a sad situation in the body of Christ today. I'm not being judgmental. I used to be in their shoes and walk their walk with one foot in the church door and the other foot outside the door. Most are highly educated in the natural physical and emotional senses of this world and have a serious lack of understanding in spiritual things. Most are only interested in what I'd call fire insurance. Just barely making it to heaven by the skin of their teeth. Most people today are more familiar with covenants through what are called contracts or paper agreements. Before discussing covenants, or the blood covenant in particular, let's have a conversation about the believers authority in Christ.

The reference scripture that is the basis of our authority is found in Luke 10: 19 (NKJV) where the Lord Jesus instructs the disciples what He has given to them,

"... authority to trample on serpents and scorpions, and over all the power of the enemy, ..."

In the same manner, we are His disciples today and He is instructing us to take and have this same authority. Ask this question - what is the substance behind the authority Jesus has delegated us? It is God the Father who is the power behind this authority. Jesus has restored the authority of Adam to believers that had been surrendered to Satan. Another verse in John 14: 13-14 Jesus again instructs the disciples to ask (demand) in His Name and He will do it in order to bring glory to the Father. God has given us 'the power of attorney' to use the Name of Jesus to meet our every need as well as the needs of others. He said,

"... whatever you ask the Father in my name He will give you." When the believer speaks in prayer, or in intercession or via a prophetic declaration in the Name of Jesus, the person is not speaking in their own name. When God the Father hears our prayer proclaimed in the Name of His Son Jesus of Nazareth, He is seeing and hearing. His Son in us. We represent our Lord Jesus as His ambassadors here on earth. The believer who completely understands that he or she has the authority of Christ in His Name with the power of God and all of heaven is backing them, they can exercise and execute their authority and face the enemy without fear.

We have that authority to use His Name. The fact that many do not use their privilege and authority is not a matter of lack of faith. They're basically ignorant of understanding their legal rights in Christ. What is evident for the most part is that believers don't understand or know about their blood covenant legal rights and privileges in Christ. They may confess and believe the promises of God a few minutes of each day, but when the rubber hits the road they lack this understanding. Ask me how I know, I've found this out for myself the hard way in my life. They don't understand that when they are reading the Bible that they are reading the words of their covenant agreement with God. Their covenant that has been signed and sealed by the blood of our Lord and Savior Jesus Christ. His Name isn't just something we tack on the end of a prayer.

Believers should grasp hold of God's purpose in establishing the blood covenant. Blood covenant practice has been part of our distant history since our creation. In our recent history, Western and European cultures have looked upon these practices as if they were barbaric and uncivilized. In our culture today, there are signs of the blood covenant that most people do not even recognize where they originated from or even know why they say them. One example would be our saying of the phrase, "... that sticks out like a sore thumb." This phrase originated from the blood covenant practice years ago of cutting the skin around the thumb and gun powder was used to rub into the wound in order to leave a mark in the incision. When the thumb healed there was a mark left by the gun powder signifying a covenant was made. Think about pierced ears and rings in the nose? Have you heard the phrase of someone saying they are "...being led around by a ring in the nose?" The ring in the nose and pierced earrings, both were considered signs of a blood covenant. The ring that is now given in marriage has replaced the practice of cutting the skin around the forefinger and marking it. Years ago, it was believed there was a blood vein that went directly from the forefinger to their heart. These are just a few of the remnant signs of blood covenant. There are many other signs and phrases we have used in our culture that have originated from blood covenants of which we have become ignorant of and they have lost all significance and meaning in our lives, specifically in the marriage covenant.

If you were to approach someone on the street today and ask them the meaning of the word covenant and you may get a varying degree of answers. Some will respond that covenants or contracts are simply made to be honored or to be broken when necessary. Many people today have a 'take it or leave it' lackadaisical attitude toward covenants. When we consider that the U.S. Constitution was setup as a covenant with the American people, look at how it has been so diluted by our courts and our government over the last 100 years or so. This alone reveals how far our western culture has fallen, and the culture doesn't have a very good track record of honoring paper contracts or agreements. Our society as a whole has long since lost their understanding of honoring covenants. A side note, non-believers do have a limited or a dulled down understanding of the fact that the life of our flesh is in the blood and there is a sacredness for life and for blood. With this understanding we have natural laws against murder.

Proceeding on to knowing the original intent of the blood covenant and how it still relates to Christian believers in our modern culture, a believer will begin to comprehend its underlying relationship and relevance to our faith and authority that comes through Christ. The blood covenant is still practiced today in various ways around the world though it has been perverted by Satan over the ages and has lost much of its relevance in the modern societies of the world. Those who have maintained the ritual are the North American Indians, South American tribes, the Caribbean and Mexican people of the Western Hemisphere. In addition, people in the Eastern Hemisphere in the remote places of Africa, the Middle East, India, Southeast Asia, Philippines, Indonesia and in Australia.

Many of the ritual practices among the various nations or people groups of the world have been described as having some similarities within the blood covenant rite or ritual.

We must keep in mind that a blood covenant is not the same as a blood sacrifice. When we read the Bible, the Old Testament has numerous scriptural references to animal sacrifices, types of animals that were allowed or not allowed for the covering of sins. In regard to when there was a covenant agreement between men, an animal sacrifice was performed on behalf of the covenant being made.

One story that comes to mind is the infamous story of Stanley & Livingstone. In short, in the late 19th century David Livingstone was a missionary to Africa and an explorer of the continent. When news of Livingstone became very scarce on his whereabouts over an extended period of six years, journalist Henry Stanley was commissioned to take an expedition to Africa in search of the missing missionary. Stanley's journey into Africa proved to have many difficulties that included sicknesses, disease, death and desertion among the members of their caravan, loss of supplies and of himself having to deal with sickness and malaria. Once the caravan had reached a certain point in their search for Livingstone, they found themselves in a troublesome situation having come in contact with a war-like tribe. At this point, Stanley's interpreter asked him why he didn't make covenant with the tribe. Stanley wasn't familiar with what this meant and discovers it meant drinking each other's blood. Stanley abhorred the thought of this ritual. But as their plight grew worse the interpreter asked him again why he refused to cut covenant. Stanley asked what could possibly be the benefit of doing this, the interpreter said, "Everything the chieftain has will be yours if you need it."

The blood covenant in Africa is mainly referred to as the covenant of strong-friendship or blood-brotherhood. There are other covenants in the world that attempt to go further with this in that they try to connect to their pagan deity. In essence, the basics of the covenant of strong friendship are when two people come together to make a sacred vow or an agreement with each other. The two parties will either clasp their hands or arms, sometimes the legs are joined, then their veins are cut and they mingle their blood together. Once they have mingled their blood, they are marked in the cut of their skin. In Stanley's case, the two covenant partners involved would each have a representative with them during the ceremony or meal who would voluntarily drink from the cup of blood being offered in covenant.

The marking of the skin was their sign or the signature of their covenant together. Many times, a covenant meal was shared among covenant parties and gifts were exchanged with each other. Articles of the agreement between them were announced for all the witnesses to hear. This announcement included the agreement (or law) of the covenant along with the blessings and the curse of this covenant. The two parties recognize the sacredness of the blood; this is a life and death covenant that cannot be annulled or dissolved. They agree to help each other in need and fight for each other unto their own death, if necessary. They are blood-brothers, meaning they are closer than family. The possessions of the first partner now belongs to their covenant partner. And whatever the second partner owns, the first partner owns as well. They live unselfishly toward each other because of their blood agreement. In a sense this reminds us of how God declared things like – "No man shall be able to stand against you; the Lord your God will put the dread of you and the fear of you upon all the land where you tread,..." (Deut. 11:25 NKJV) Covenants originated with God from the beginning! God still is a God of covenant and the Bible was written by the Holy Spirit to give us record of our covenant.

Now, if one of the covenant parties chooses to violate their blood covenant, then the one who violates it better be on watch for his own life. Breaking of the covenant means death for the one in violation. In some cases, it has been known to happen where several generations of family will hunt down the covenant violator and take their life for the penalty of breaking the blood covenant. Life and death are associated with this covenant. Knowing this allows us to understand this type of covenant is actually a direct descendent from when God cut the covenant with Abraham indicated in Genesis chapter 15.

From Stanley's story noted above, it is a little humorous in that as he was covenanting with the chieftain, he was worried about his stomach condition because the chieftain asked for his goat in the covenant exchange of gifts. Stanley drank goat's milk for his stomach condition and did not initially want to give up his goat. All he received from the chieftain was what appeared to be a worthless 7-foot-long copper-wound spear. Stanley thought he got the short end of the deal in their exchange. But once Stanley took the spear on his journey, he began to realize the continent of Africa opened up to him. As he carried that spear, the tribes they encountered would bow in submission to him. Stanley came to understand that in order to survive and walk in safety in the continent of Africa, they had to observe and participate in what they thought was a primitive and barbaric practice of covenanting with blood.

Believers need to understand in this type of relationship is that blood is truly a sacred and precious thing. Blood itself not what is holy about this type of agreement. The blood is only the sign or signature of the covenant represented in the exchange of each other's life. The holy things in the covenant are the words. Words can cause life and words can cause death. We know this from Proverbs 18:21. Even Jesus said "... the words I speak to you are spirit and they are life ..." found in John 6:63. Our words carry a lot of weight in both the spiritual and physical realms, whether we recognize this or not. In Matthew 12:37 Jesus said, "For by your words you will be justified, and by your words you will be condemned." Words of the covenant are holy.

Of course, believers should recognize that all of the blood related rituals taking place around the world are Satanic perversions of what God started in the beginning at the Garden of Eden after Adam and Eve had sinned. It's recorded as follows -

> Genesis 3:21 (NKJV) "Also for Adam and his wife the Lord God made tunics of skin, and clothed them."

We can see from this one verse that God initiated and made the first covenant with Adam and Eve through the blood sacrifice of animals. With this he provided their clothes for covering their nakedness and the blood covered for their sin. Hebrews 9:22 says that without the shedding of blood there is no remission or atonement for sin. In the book of Job, we read Job had a covenant of life that was only for himself. For some unknown reason it didn't include his wife or kids. We understand this because God tells Satan he could not take Job's life. In Genesis 15, we are introduced to the Abrahamic covenant. Through this blood covenant, we read where God himself cuts the covenant of strong-friendship and swears an oath to Abraham. God told Abraham to sacrifice and cut certain animals and lay the pieces on the ground. God Himself then walks between the sacrificed animals and announces their blood agreement. Once this happened, Abraham became strong friend of God. And vice versa. This blood covenant was just as serious on God's side of this agreement. If He ever broke the covenant, He would have had to destroy Himself. The Bible says that He swore by Himself, because there was no one or nothing higher that He could swear by. In Psalms, it says He holds the integrity of His word in a higher regard than Himself. His word is His bond. He will not violate His word. A blood covenant was more than just an agreement or contract on a piece of paper. The blood covenant was not made lightly and it was not made to where it could be broken later on. It was a life and death agreement, with blessings and curses. This is hard for our modern mind to comprehend, but the beauty of this is that God chose to do this for Abraham to help him in his faith.

You'll notice that God will always provide a substitute for the blood sacrifice. The only blood requirement God placed on Abraham in their agreement was to have Abraham circumcise himself and all in his household, including his seed after him as a sign of his everlasting covenant.

The blood covenant was given by God for man to understand the strongest possible agreement includes both life and death between each participant of the agreement to indicate just how serious it was with

Him. And when this type of covenant was initially instituted by God, we don't find any drinking of blood or where the blood passes by the lips of a man. In fact, God made it a law in the Old Covenant that the drinking of blood was forbidden and it still is to this day. Understand that if it is witnessed today where the drinking of blood takes place in any ceremony or in covenant, it is not of God but a perversion of Satan. There were specific instructions given in the Old Covenant to show proper respect for blood that was shed whether it be from animal sacrifice, in hunt for food and the unfortunate death or killing of people. The life of the flesh is in the blood. If you recall the Genesis 4:10 account of when Cain murdered Abel, God says, "What have you done? The voice of your brother's blood cries out to Me from the ground." (NKJV) Apparently, blood has a voice that speaks in the spiritual realm because of the life that is contained within it originated from God, who is spirit and life.

On the other hand, God doesn't have a need to have blood shed to make Him honest in keeping covenant. God is honorable and truthful. He is not like a man that He should lie (Num. 23:19). We discover in Psalm 138:2 that God exalts His word higher than himself. Once God has spoken, spiritual law is established. The main reason God uses blood in a covenant agreement, it's because man recognizes that blood is sacred and the fact that the life of our flesh is in our blood. This was to let men know how serious it is when people approach a blood-honored and blood-spilled agreement. Through this blood agreement with Abraham an everlasting covenant was established with the Creator of the universe!

Let's look closer at another aspect of God's covenant with Abraham in Genesis 22: 1-19 (NKJV) –

'Now it came to pass after these things that God tested Abraham, and said to him, "Abraham!" And he said, "Here I am." Then He said, "Take now your son, your only son Isaac, whom you love, and go to the land of Moriah, and offer him there as a burnt offering on one of the mountains of which I shall tell you." So Abraham rose early in the morning and saddled his donkey, and took two of his young men with him, and Isaac his son; and he split the wood for the burnt offering, and arose and went to the place of which God had told him. Then on the third day Abraham lifted his eyes and saw the place afar off. And Abraham said to his young men, "Stay here with the donkey; the lad and I will go yonder and worship, and we will come back to you." So, Abraham took the wood of the burnt offering and laid it on Isaac his son; and he took the fire in his hand, and a knife, and the two of them went together. But Isaac spoke to Abraham his father and said, "My father!" And he said, "Here I am, my son." Then he said, "Look, the fire and the wood, but where is the lamb for a burnt offering?" And Abraham said, "My son, God will provide for Himself the lamb for a burnt offering." So the two of them went together. Then they came to the place of which God had told him. And Abraham built an altar there and placed the wood in order; and he bound Isaac his son and laid him on the altar, upon the wood. And Abraham stretched out his hand and took the knife to slay his son. But the Angel of the Lord called to him from heaven and said, "Abraham, Abraham!" So he said, "Here I am." And He said, "Do not lay your hand on the lad, or do anything to him; for now I know that you fear God, since you have not withheld your son, your only son, from Me." Then Abraham lifted his eyes and looked, and there behind him was a ram caught in a thicket by its horns. So Abraham went and took the ram, and offered it up for a burnt offering instead of his son. And Abraham called the name of the place, The-Lord-Will-Provide (Jehovah-Jireh); as it is said to this day, "In the Mount of the Lord it shall be provided." Then the Angel of the Lord called to Abraham a second time out of heaven, and said: "By Myself I have sworn, says the Lord, because you have done this thing, and have not withheld your son, your only son— blessing I will bless you, and multiplying I will multiply your descendants as the stars of the heaven and as the sand which is on the seashore; and your descendants shall possess the gate of their enemies. In your seed all the nations of the earth shall be blessed, because you have obeyed My voice." So Abraham returned to his young men, and they rose and went together to Beersheba; and Abraham dwelt at Beersheba.'

This event would allow Abraham to reason within himself and have strong faith that God was going to raise Isaac from the dead because God's promise to him included his seed through Isaac. (Hebrews 11) God and Abraham's agreement was signed and sealed by blood! Their agreement required that God would be obligated to raise Isaac from the dead if Abraham's knife had struck his son. Once God saw the faithfulness of Abraham to follow through, He provided a substitute sacrifice and told Abraham to stay his hand from striking Isaac – his only son. (Genesis 22) Ishmael was not the son of God's of promise to Abraham. Isaac was the son of promise. In fact, before this sacrifice, Abraham called "those things that be not as though they were" in that he told Isaac that God would provide the sacrifice when there was none. And he had told the servants that he and Isaac would return. Not only was this a faith statement from Abraham, his actions as a blood-covenant partner obligated God the Father to also offer up His only Son when He came into the earth. The faith actions of the covenant partner friend of God obligates God to send His Son Jesus, who becomes the final blood sacrifice for all of us.

In Paul's letter to the Galatians – Chapter 3, he writes that through Abraham's covenant, Gentile believers are also included in Abraham's covenant blessings through the cross of Christ. The curse from sin, sickness, disease, and death has been removed by the precious blood that flowed for us. Not only are believers made a strong friend of God through faith, but are in a new covenant position with Christ that brings us into the throne room of God. Seated with Christ in heavenly places. The new covenant through the blood of Christ provides for us an everlasting covenant of adoption, joint heirs with Christ, including being made a son/daughter of God. His blood is sacred, His word is sacred and we have been privileged as believers to boldly come to His throne of grace to receive mercy in our hour of need. God is no longer on the outside looking in, Jesus provides the new and living way into the throne room of God, through His blood. All honor, power and praise to God!

Take a moment to consider the blood of Jesus and what it represents. What is faith in the blood of Jesus? Or faith in Jesus' blood? If a believer is stopped on the street somewhere and asked – "Do you have faith in the blood of Jesus? Most church goers would answer, "Oh, yes! I do!" Then if they were asked in the next breath – "What does having faith in His blood mean?" Many would just unknowingly stare into space. Why is there power in the blood? What is the difference between atoning and remission blood? Should believers in Christ know and be familiar with the meaning of these things? The answer is 'yes.'

Sadly, most do not have a clue about these nor a clue as to what is ours in Christ. If you want to stir the pot – just mention to someone, "Jesus' blood did not atone for sin." Understand this clearly, if His blood merely atoned for sin, then His blood is no more sacred than the blood of a bull or a goat. (Hebrews 10:3-4) The blood of an animal "atones" for sin. "Atone" simply means to cover. Religious doctrine has been ingrained within the whole worldwide church body to believe atonement comes through the blood of Christ. They've mistakenly applied the Hebrew word that is translated into the English word 'atone' or 'atonement.' To be fair and it's unfortunate, there's one scripture in the New Testament (KJV) regarding the blood of Jesus that uses or has the word "atonement" (Rom.5:11). The word remission should have been used, in lieu of atonement. The NKJV uses the word reconciliation. It's the only place in the New Testament (KJV) where it can be found. Jesus' blood did not simply cover our sin. Jesus' blood destroyed the authority and dominion of sin that was over us in order to set us totally free! Remission means 'to send away,' it signifies a release from bondage or imprisonment, a dismissal, sending away, and forgiveness, with the added benefit of canceling out all judgement, punishment, obligation, or debt. Sin is defeated! (Remission - Matthew 26:28; Mark 1:4; Luke 1:77 & 24:27; Hebrews 9:22 & 10:18, and Acts 10:43)

Remission is one of the great words of the new covenant. God has remitted our sin; they are wiped out as though they had never existed. The word "remission" is never used but in connection with the new birth. Before we come to Christ, we are approaching Him as a sinner. When we heard the good news of the gospel and took Christ as our Lord and Savior, confessed Him as our Lord, then all of the sin that we had ever done is completely wiped out. In the new birth our spirit is changed and, in our spirit, a new creation takes the place of the old. After we become Christians, we have our sins forgiven based on our new relationship and the intercession of Christ on our behalf. Several times the same Greek word translated for 'remission' is translated as 'forgiveness' in the New Testament. In Ephesians 1:7 (NKJV) it says, "In whom (Christ) we have our redemption through His blood, the remission of our trespasses." Read also Col. 1:13-14; Acts 26:18. The remission of our sins replaces the blood of the scapegoat sacrificed under the Old Covenant. This scapegoat carried away the sins of the people once a year, while the blood that was shed covered Israel as a nation. Through the blood of Christ, our sins are remitted completely and we are re-created in spirit. Forgiveness and remission are relationship words based upon a new covenant New Testament perspective.

When a sinner accepts Christ as Savior, his spirit is re-created, his sins are remitted, but if he remains ignorant of what has happened to him, he will always remain conscious of sin. On the ground of his relationship as a child of God, and Jesus' intercessory and advocate ministry sitting at the right hand of the Father, there is ground for forgiveness for the sin that is committed. 1John Chapters 1 and 2 deal with this great issue of forgiveness. When a child of God commits sin, he breaks his fellowship with the Father. He does not break his relationship. He merely breaks the fellowship, much like what happens when a husband and wife argue and say unkind words to each other. It ruins the fellowship of the home, but that can be restored by the willing process of both parties to forgive and to repent. The same holds true between a Christian and God the Father. The moment that we recognize our sin and the fellowship with the Father has been broken, if we confess our sin and repent in the Name of Jesus, God the Father is faithful and righteous to forgive us our sin and to cleanse us from all unrighteousness.

> In 1John 2:1-2, (NKJV) it says, "My little children, these things I write unto you that you may not sin. And if anyone sins, we have an Advocate with the Father, Jesus Christ the righteous."

Many Christians today, who are living in broken fellowship, would be living victorious lives in Christ if they knew that Jesus was their Advocate. Because of our unrenewed minds and the constant battle of Satanic persuasion in our minds, we sometimes sin and cause our fellowship with the Father to be broken. Every child of God who breaks fellowship with the Father comes under condemnation. If he had no advocate to plead his case before the Father he would be in a sad position. The word shows us that if we do sin we have an advocate with the Father. Let's consider the meaning of the word "advocate."

> In Webster's dictionary we read: "1. One who pleads the cause of another. Specifically: One who pleads the cause of another before a tribunal or judicial court; a counselor. 2. One who defends, vindicates, or espouses any cause by argument; a pleader; as, an advocate of free trade, an advocate of truth. 3. Christ, considered as an intercessor. To plead in favor of; to defend by argument, before a tribunal or the public; to support, vindicate, or recommend publicly."

Christ is our defender, our upholder. He is always there, at the right hand of God, ready to come to our aid ... to intercede on our behalf. In 1John 1:3-9, it indicates God's method for maintaining our fellowship with Him. If we sin so that our fellowship is broken, we may renew that fellowship by confessing our sin and to repent, by turning from and casting it away from us.

When a person accepts Christ as Lord and Savior, they become a new child of God. At this moment, Christ begins His intercessory work. Jesus is mediator for the sinner, but He is intercessor for the Christian. There are some who may ask: "Why does a believer need an intercessor? Especially the intercession that comes from Christ?" The answer to that is found in Romans 12:2. In our new birth, our spirits receive the life of God. The next step in our walk is that our minds need to be renewed. Before Christ, we walked as natural men, a son of disobedience, Satan ruled our minds. Once our spirits have received the life of God, our natural minds must be renewed by the word of God so that we will know our privileges and responsibilities as children of God. When we apply His word to renewing our mind, it will change the way we think and change our worldview to a biblical worldview. His thoughts become our thoughts. The new birth is instantaneous, but the renewing of our mind is a gradual process that we as individual Christians must diligently do for our own good and survival. Our growth in Christ is determined by our study and meditation in His word. During our life on earth we need the intercession of Christ in our behalf to finish our course. Many times we strain our fellowship with the Father, as in our ignorance of His will, we many times say and do things that are not pleasing to Him.

Then again, we need His intercession, because we have to come to a place of understanding our authority in Christ. New babes in Christ do not begin their walk and life in Christ in full maturity. The Christian life is a process of growth and maturity.

> Hebrews 7:25 (NKJV) says "Therefore He (Christ) is also able to save to the uttermost those who come to God through Him, since He always lives to make intercession for them."

After a brief detour, let's track back toward the direction and discussion of the blood of Christ. In the book of Hebrews, the remission of sin and atonement of sin are compared clearly revealing the sacrifice of Christ purges our conscience in remission, which is from having a sin conscience over to having a clear conscience. Why does the Name of Jesus have power? Again, most do not know – it is because of the blood! The world-wide church has been ignorant of why we cannot get anyone delivered from their sickness or physical condition, or whatever it may be! What happens many times when there are healings that occur, they're more like an act of mercy from the Father. Because of no knowledge and being strangers from the covenants of promise, not knowing why the blood of Jesus is powerful, not knowing the authority that comes by that blood using His Name in resisting the devil and destroying his works! We are blood covenant partners with God Almighty who has given authority to us by the new blood covenant cut in the Lamb of God's flesh and His blood flowed for our benefit!

A warning - if we would realize and wake up to how we live our daily lives, if we did – then I don't think we would dare bring an accusation nor cause an argument with the pastor or the leadership in the local church. Wouldn't dare speak anything contrary to God's word about one of our blood-bought Christian brethren to cause them to fall or into sin. We should bite our tongue before we speak raising our voice to come against another child of the living God, because we have cut the covenant with them in the partaking of the Lord 's table. Becoming unified together in the sharing of His body and blood. That is the reason it's called in the New Testament – 'communion,' this word means, 'our fellowship together in the blood of the Lamb.' We have raised the cup of the covenant together. The church has done this so ignorantly that the Bible says when we do it unworthily – it can harm us! That's a powerful and a very unpleasant statement. And we go on about our lives and can't figure out 'why!' are so many Christians are sick, broke, down and diseased in their bodies and in their minds! They have no comprehension of what that table is and what it represents! It is so much more than just a tiny cup of grape juice and a fake little wafer!

For many years of my life, I was convinced that there was something about the Last Supper of the Lord's table that I did not understand. At the time no one could explain it. Always wondered why we had to recite the Lord's instructions, why we had to drink grape juice and eat a stale cracker or a wafer. And I also spent many years wondering why on earth would God ever require and allow all those barbaric and gross animal blood sacrifices. When I was younger, I did not understand and it confused me greatly. You could say that I was definitely "a stranger and foreigner to the covenants of promise" as noted in Ephesians Chapter 2. For a long time, I wondered, "What was the underlying principle behind all these strange practices?" The very language of Jesus, when He said, "Verily, verily, [or Truly, Truly] I say unto you, except you eat of the flesh of the Son of Man, and drink His blood, you have no life in you," (NKJV) this added to my confusion. It was repulsive and sounded much like cannibalism to me.

What did He mean by all of this? Well, let us review this last statement by Jesus in the context of His message to the disciples in John Chapter 6 (NKJV) starting in vs. 22 (this is after the feeding of the five thousand –

"..., they also got into boats and came to Capernaum, seeking Jesus. And when they found Him on the other side of the sea, they said to Him, Rabbi, when did You come here? Jesus answered them and said, Most assuredly, I say to you, you seek Me, not because you saw the signs, but because you ate of the loaves and were filled. Do not labor for the food which perishes, but for the food which endures to everlasting life, which the Son of Man will give you, because God the Father has set His seal on Him. Then they said to Him, What shall we do, that we may work the works of God? Jesus answered and said to them, This is the work of God, that you believe in Him whom He sent. Therefore they said to Him, What sign will You perform then, that we may see it and believe You? What work will You do? Our fathers ate the manna in the desert; as it is written, 'He gave them bread from heaven to eat. Then Jesus said to them, Most assuredly, I say to you, Moses did not give you the bread from heaven, but My Father gives you the true bread from heaven. For the bread of God is He who comes down from heaven and gives life to the world. Then they said to Him, Lord, give us this bread always. And Jesus said to them, I am the bread of life. He who comes to Me shall never hunger, and he who believes in Me shall never thirst. But I said to you that you have seen Me and yet do not believe. All that the Father gives Me will come to Me, and the one who comes to Me I will by no means cast out. For I have come down from heaven, not to do My own will, but the will of Him who sent Me. This is the will of the Father who sent Me, that of all He has given Me I should lose nothing, but should raise it up at the last day. And this is the will of Him who sent Me, that everyone who sees the Son and believes in Him may have everlasting life; and I will raise him up at the last day. The Jews then complained about Him, because He said, I am the bread which came down from heaven. And they said, Is not this Jesus, the son of Joseph, whose father and mother we know? How is it then that He says, I have come down from heaven? Jesus therefore answered and said to them, Do not murmur among yourselves. No one can come to Me unless the Father who sent Me draws him; and I will raise him up at the last day. It is written in the prophets, And they shall all be taught by God. Therefore, everyone who has heard and learned from the Father comes to Me. Not that anyone has seen the Father, except He who is from God; He has seen the Father. Most assuredly, I say to you, he who believes in Me has everlasting life. I am the bread of life. Your fathers ate the manna in the wilderness, and are dead. This is the bread which comes down from heaven, that one may eat of it and not die. I am the living bread which came down from heaven. If anyone eats of this bread, he will live forever; and the bread that I shall give is My flesh, which I shall give for the life of the world. The Jews therefore quarreled among themselves, saying, How can this Man give us His flesh to eat? Then Jesus said to them, Most assuredly, I say to you, unless you eat the flesh of the Son of Man and drink His blood, you have no life in you. Whoever eats My flesh and drinks My blood has eternal life, and I will raise him up at the last day. For My flesh is food indeed, and My blood is drink indeed. He who eats My flesh and drinks My blood abides in Me, and I in him. As the living Father sent Me, and I live because of the Father, so he who feeds on Me will live because of Me. This is the bread which came down from heaven—not as your fathers ate the manna, and are dead. He who eats this bread will live forever. These things He said in the synagogue as He taught in Capernaum. Therefore many of His disciples, when they heard this, said, This is a hard saying; who can understand it? When Jesus knew in Himself that His disciples complained about this, He said to them, Does this offend you? What then if you should see the Son of Man ascend where He was before? It is the Spirit who gives life; the flesh profits nothing. The words that I speak to you are spirit, and they are life.(vs.63)

What does Jesus mean by saying all of this? He is revealing and professing the new blood covenant to them in a parable, and they could not recognize nor understand it. Recall that it was John who revealed in the beginning of his Gospel account, Jesus was the Word of God made flesh and who dwelled among us. In Chapter 6, Jesus equates the eating of His flesh and the drinking of His blood with abiding, dwelling, and living in Him through the consumption of His word into our very being, by hearing with our ears, our minds, and our spirits, allowing it to engulf our entire being. This revelation from Jesus is the declaration and the soon to be institution of what becomes known as the new covenant table of the Lord.

In Exodus 12 we read where God instituted the annual ritual meal of Passover before their departure from Egypt and the plague of death upon the firstborn. All the children of Israel were to sacrifice the lamb of a goat or a sheep, to place the blood of the lamb on the lintel above and the side door posts, to get dressed and be prepared to leave Egypt, then to roast the lamb and to eat all of it. When the death angel came near, the blood marked the homes to be left alone and he passed over, while those who had no blood mark were visited and where a death occurred. The Israelites were to make this an annual ritual of remembrance of God's deliverance from their slavery and bondage in Egypt. Israel only viewed this meal as a ritual of remembrance, but this sacrificial meal was a blood covenant of deliverance to be remembered throughout the generations to come.

Later in three of the Gospel accounts, during this Passover meal we find Jesus is with the disciples gathered the night before the Crucifixion. The following is a paraphrase, Jesus says to them, "I long to break this bread with you and drink this cup"; and after He had blessed the bread and broke it, He said, "Take and eat, this is My body which is broken for you." Then He took the cup of wine and said, "Take and drink, this is My Blood of the new covenant that is poured out for many unto the remission of sins."

Notice the silence of the disciples during these moments when Jesus introduced this, saying "This is my blood of the new covenant, which is poured out for many unto the remission of sins"; and then told them to eat the bread which was His body and to drink the wine which He declared was His blood, the very silence of the disciples indicates they understood what he meant. They knew their covenant history and the Passover event by heart. They knew that when they drank from the cup of the new covenant with Jesus in the upper room that night, they were entering into the strongest, most sacred covenant known to mankind. If we know anything about the Passover table, there is an extra cup on the table that is mostly referred to as the cup of Elijah, which is also in reference to the Messiah Himself. No one ever before and up to that time ever drank from this cup. It was placed there for the Messiah to come. The disciples kept noticeably and seriously silent because Jesus was passing the bread representing His flesh and the cup of the Messiah around the group to drink from it together with Him for the establishment of the new covenant relationship. They had never seen nor heard of this ever being done before.

This has been passed down to us, we have been given the communion table of the Lord's supper, where we are now participants to remember and recognize His blood covenant with us. Through His blood, Christ gives us the honor, the right and privilege of taking His Name as our own with all the authority and power that is behind that Name. The Father sees Jesus in us. The great exchange of His life in us and our life in Him. As Jesus prayed, we become one with Him and one with the Father through Him (John 17).

> Hebrews 8: 6 (NKJV) says that Jesus is the "... Mediator of a better covenant, established on better promises." And in 2Corinthians 1: 20 (NKJV) it says ",,, For all the promises of God in Him (Christ) are Yes, and in Him Amen, to the glory of God through us."

So, when we read the Bible, especially the New Testament, we are really reading the words of our new covenant that came through Christ. If we will awaken to this fact and realize that we walk and live under a new covenant guaranteed by the body, the blood, the life, and resurrection of Jesus our Lord. It is warranted and is guaranteed by His very existence. As we hear and read His word aloud, it becomes sacred to us and His promises come alive inside us by the power of Holy Spirit. Hearing the word should stir our faith and trust in God.

If Jesus was willing to follow through and fulfill God's plan of redemption that included making a blood covenant through His own sacrificial blood and bound himself to the covenant and the promises within His word, why should we as believers hold anything back from Him when it comes to our commitment to Him. Why should we not consider ourselves to be bound to Him through His blood and live our life surrendered to Him completely. This is part of the reason the Apostle Paul identifies himself as a 'bond-servant' of Christ. Given this understanding, we should pledge our unqualified commitment to Jesus as Lord and Savior, and allow the Holy Spirit to empower and enable us into the greater works that Jesus mentions in the Gospel of John. This is a blood-based relationship with Him.

As we come alive to this revelation, our faithfulness and obedience to Him will appropriate the covenant blessing of Abraham. In Deuteronomy 28, the blessings of Abraham are listed there. Blessed coming in, blessed going out, blessing from the work of our hands, protection, prosperity, and divine healing, just to name a few. The curses that are also listed there no longer apply to us per Galatians Chapter 3. Our authority and power are in speaking and using the Name of Jesus that is above our own name. The Father authorizes us to use His Name because through His blood and His Name we are grafted into His body and have become part of His family. Jesus is our Lord and we represent Him on the earth until His return.

Now comes the fun part in our conversation regarding the subject of Prayer. For most new converts and many believers today, prayer is a difficult thing to do. Mostly it stems from a lack of understanding spiritual things. You may ask me how I know, because I remember my early years of difficulty and admittedly, I am still learning and growing in this endeavor. Most people look at prayer to God as the same as their relationship with their own earthly fathers. If their relationship was good with their earthly father, then they may develop a descent prayer life with the heavenly Father. If their relationship was the opposite, then more than likely their prayer life is going to struggle. I can attest to this situation in my own life. Although I had a stepdad most of my childhood who helped my mom raise me, I can tell you his heart was not completely there for a relationship with me. My biological dad was not around and there was truly no father figure relationship to rely upon. When my stepdad became a believer, I knew there were some changes in him and it had an influence in my life. But, even after salvation, there was an emotional and relational distance between us.

I now know that he did the best he could for what he knew during that time. I am not writing this part to use as an excuse for the lack of a prayer life, but I can say over a long period of time in the past this relationship had an ill effect in how I related and communicated with my heavenly Father and my own family. But this can be overcome via mind renewal with the word of God and help from Holy Spirit.

The subject of prayer is always met with some basic resistance and some ignorance in that most people, including a lot of Christians, who do not know God as a true Father. Most of them have a skewed mental view of a traditional religious God who mainly prefers to keep His distance and have very little to do with us on earth. And, that those who do pray, say their prayers like darts thrown at a dart board in order that He may choose to answer one of them on a day of His choosing, or maybe occasionally, if at all. They struggle worse in relating to the Father in Heaven because of their lack of familiarity with Him. On the other hand, sadly many Christians really do not place much value on learning or knowing how to pray properly. They have difficulty grasping hold of things relating to the Spirit. There are some who have a fear of praying. If Christians would just wake up and dedicate themselves to spend quality time in the Word of God, they would recognize there are prayers within God's word they can learn for themselves. In addition, they would learn there are benefits from God from praying in faith through love. Discovering His will is in His word, and when we pray according to His word and will, we can trust and rest in Him that He is working for us in our behalf.

In simple terms, the meaning of the word prayer implies communicating with the Father and that there are many different types of prayer described in God's word. The best description of prayer that I have heard in a recent message was that prayer is more like communion or fellowship with the Father, in lieu of just talking to Him. Jesus offered some insight to the disciples on what is referred to as the Model Prayer or the Lord's Prayer found in (Matt. 6: 9-15) that is a great starting point in all our prayers to the Heavenly Father. But it is His comments regarding how to approach our Father that are noted prior to the Lord's Prayer that I have put into practice for my own use during my quiet time with the Father.

> Matt. 6: 6 (NKJV) 'But you, when you pray, go into your room, and when you have shut your door, pray to your Father who is in the secret place; and your Father who sees in secret will reward you openly.' He (Jesus) tells us two things to do in this verse. First is 'go into your room.'

Find a place where you can get private with the Lord. Second, shut the door. When you go into your room, you get away from the world; when you shut the door, you get away from the family. Shutting the door indicates that you are really going to get private – just you and God. No one else can see what is going on. When you are in private, He says to 'pray to your Father who is in the secret place; and your Father who sees in secret will reward you openly.' Again, the word 'openly' here indicates there are even natural rewards for prayer. The prayer of faith can get you healed; Prayer to the Father can bring finances for you; can provide things that you need here in this life. So, prayer does bring about rewards that can be seen and provided in the natural realm. Prayer is primarily directed to our Father.

> Matt. 6: 7-8 (NKJV) 'And when you pray, do not use vain repetitions, as the heathen do. For they think that they will be heard for their many words. Therefore, do not be like them. For your Father knows the things you have need of before you ask Him.'

Your heavenly Father knows what you have need of, but the Word of God also tells us to put Him in remembrance of His Word. (Isaiah 43: 26) To put God in remembrance of His Word, we must know His

Word first. '...faith comes by hearing, and hearing by the Word of God (Romans 10:17).' Therefore, to have faith (in prayer), you must have some working knowledge of the Word of God."

These scriptures and the attitude in which Jesus is teaching His disciples speaks volumes and speaks directly to my heart in that my personality type prefers to not be out in front of people looking for attention. I enjoy this private time of meditation and prayer in the early mornings.

Regarding prayers that tend to be off track or amiss in the Christian world today, I have thoughts of concern for all the baby Christians learning bad habits along the way as they grow in the Lord. One of the major concerns is the practice of "binding and loosing" along with misunderstanding of the scripture referencing the "keys of the kingdom" and finally misunderstanding our authority in Christ.

As an example, I should clarify that this occurs mostly during group gathering prayer times with either home cell groups or with church prayer teams during church services. In their attempts to speak with authority over some circumstance, or sickness or for a specific situation, the words "bind and loose" tend to be used and directed at our enemy the devil and his cohorts. My heartfelt opinion is that we are praying/asking and speaking "amiss" in this area. Some may say that this opinion may be somewhat anal, and many tend to excuse themselves saying God knows their heart and knows what they mean when they pray. To some extent this is true, but after some time of study and prayer, I am becoming more convinced many of us are amiss.

My comments are not to ridicule our prayers, but another area of being amiss is regarding prayer chains. Many believers in numerous denominations and non-denominations have developed a certain habit of the joining together of as many people as possible for prayer requests. They tend to think if they pull on enough people, or a large group of known prayer warriors believing that if enough of these prayers are offered, they will somehow finally reach God's ear in heaven.

Normally, many of these prayers are intended for some immediate need or in many cases intended for a healing miracle from God. Sometimes even non-believers who accept the prayers of believers will invite or grant this type of request. Please don't misunderstand, I'm all about prayer and the type of prayers that are without ceasing (1 Thess. 5:17). The main problem we run into with this is continually making the same requests over and over and over again. Other scriptures that teach on prayer instruct us to avoid repetitive prayers and begging type prayers. Jesus taught that when we pray, to have faith in God and to believe we have received the answer (Mark 11:22-24). The meaning of "have faith in God" is intended for us to trust God completely, taking Him at His word. It's another way of saying that we take God's word on the situation as the only truth and stand firm in it. Afterward, we thank Him in our prayers for hearing our prayers and answering them because we pray according to His will and His word. Jesus also taught that when two or three are gathered together in His Name, He is there in our midst with us (Matt. 18: 20). It doesn't necessarily take more than two or three people for agreement in prayer. In addition, since we live in the New Testament age, believers have been raised up together, and made to sit together in the heavenly places in Christ Jesus (Eph. 2: 6). We should understand and recognize we are already in the throne room of God's grace (Heb. 4:16). Shouting up to and begging God is unnecessary. Another way of looking at this is - if you are born-again, Christ is in you and you are in Him (John 17).

Another area that is especially touchy or a religious area for most people that occurs during our prayer times of binding and loosing of our enemy for all the bad situations in life. Since God's word is the final authority in all we are to say and do, and if Jesus is our true example to walk as He walked, then I would say this type of prayer or speaking out appears scripturally incorrect. Believers are instructed to "resist" the devil. We are not instructed to have a devil binding and loosing prayer meeting. We resist the enemy and sin by living in our authority in the Name of Jesus and standing upon the Word of God, then he flees.

Remember the temptation of Jesus in the wilderness. He resisted the devil standing on and speaking the Word of God in authority and by the enabling power of the Holy Spirit. There was no binding and loosing being spoken. After the temptation, we read the gospel accounts of Jesus ministry on earth and the follow-up ministry of the disciples and of Paul in the book of Acts. If Jesus ever spoke to the demons to "come out" of the possessed, it was briefly spoken with authority. He spoke once and did not repeat himself. He did not waste time or His words. When He prayed, it was mostly alone and He always directed His prayers to the Father. In Acts, Paul only spoke to the spirit in the annoying girl from Philippi "to come out of her in the Name of Jesus."

Regarding Jesus' statement about the Keys of the Kingdom found in Matthew 16:19, it is simply based on the authority that has been returned to those who choose to believe in Him and in His Name. He said, "...whatever you bind on earth will be bound in heaven, whatever you loose on earth will be loosed in heaven." He is identifying the authority Adam had lost in the beginning. This authority has now been returned to those who choose to believe in Him. In John 17, Jesus praying to the Father, "...He in the Father, the Father in Him, (then He said) He in us, that all of us may be one in Him!" Therefore, whatever believers say and do on the earth (with Christ in them) and having authority to live and use the Name of Jesus, then what we say and do is also settled in heaven, because He is in us and we are in Him. Jesus does not mention anything about prayer.

Another area is related. Mainly during prayers against any sickness. Again, the prayer is usually including a "binding and loosing of our enemy." Yes, in Acts, it says Jesus came to destroy the works of the devil. We can read all about what those works were. Most of the time, Jesus either spoke directly to the fevers, or infirmity, or told people their faith made them well. Several times the Father's compassion simply moved Jesus to heal the multitude or raise the dead. In addition, Peter and Paul also were led in the Spirit in the same manner as Jesus when dealing with sickness and disease. Not just because they were somehow special or had an exclusive anointing, no disrespect intended. All believers are anointed and are allowed to lay hands on the sick for their recovery. Many of these were direct and to the point. There is only one instance recorded in Luke 13: 12-16 where Jesus saw the woman, He called her to Him and said to her, "Woman, you are loosed from your infirmity." And He laid His hands on her, and immediately she was made straight, and glorified God. Then He demanded an answer from the synagogue rulers because it was the Sabbath, on whether this covenant daughter of Abraham ought to be loosed from her bond (or infirmity) who had been bound by Satan for 18 years. They went away ashamed. In reference to the words of bound and loosed, they were not used in any way in a prayer. They were words of authority spoken in the power of the Holy Spirit. Jesus spoke to the woman, not to Satan.

Presently, I do not believe there were a lot of prayers for sickness at that time. On the other hand, in our day and hour, this has evolved in Christian circles into an attitude of "pray over and about everything." I am becoming convinced that this may not be completely correct or that prayer is necessary all the time in all situations. The scripture does not say pray an hour or two while you are laying hands on the sick. In our prayer times, we do not need to "bind and loose" the enemy from our lives. Signs and wonders are supposed to follow those who believe. In other words, be prayed up before we lay our hands on the sick. Be like Jesus and walk as He walked.

I believe we have mistakenly assumed that we are somehow allowed to make the devil our whipping boy, but I do not see where we are to give him any recognition, any credit, any glory, any of our prayer time or any attention. Giving him attention only distracts us and draws our attention away from the Father. We are to be cognizant of thoughts from the enemy, his deceptions, and attacks. We resist him by setting our focus on drawing near to God through His Word, in doing so, God draws near to us.

There is another instance we read where Paul was hindered by Satan when he wanted to travel to another country. We do not read where Paul is binding and loosening the devil from that situation so he could continue his travel without being impeded. There were reasons for the hindrance. That is why we are to be Spirit-led in our lives, not to be head-led, desire-led or emotion-led.

There is another phrase that has been used very loosely in our circles, "I believe in the Power of Prayer." Truthfully, prayer has no power. It is possible to pray amiss our entire life. What is true, the power manifests (is revealed) during our prayers when we are in the presence of God the Father. When we pray in accordance with His will, this is when His power and presence are manifested. In my humble opinion, this is having communion with the Father, our Lord Jesus, and Holy Spirit. If there is one area of agreement regarding the issue of binding and loosing, that is taking authority over our own flesh in the following example –

> "Father, I repent of holding on to bad feelings toward others. I bind myself to godly repentance and loose myself from bitterness, resentment, envying, strife, and unkindness ... I choose to forgive and release them..."

When I was a young Christian, prayer seemed difficult and hard because it sounded like I was just talking to the air and hearing myself stumble over the words I spoke. Honestly, I hated it. I did not realize until much later in life that God hears us when we pray according to His will. (1John 5:14) And His word is His will. Which in turn meant that I had to get to know what was in His word that related to me. I soon discovered Father God has our best interests at heart and learned

He loves all of us just as much as He loved Jesus. This process requires time and learning.

A phrase that has stuck with me ever since I heard it, "If you ever want to have God speak to you, you have to have an intimate relationship with His word." The scripture says as you draw near to Him, then He will draw near to you. Once you discover this, you will start to have thoughts and a certain knowing on the inside of you that it is the Holy Spirit speaking back to you in your spirit. Yes, He will respond and He speaks through our Conscience. I mentioned this earlier in the first chapter. I do not mean you will hear an audible voice. Most of the time it will be a "knowing" inside you. Sometimes it will be just a word or a thought brought to your mind. Other times you will have "peace" in you. Sometimes you will be led of the Spirit by what "seems" or "appears" good." Then there will be times of hearing a small still voice inside. But you must understand that these leadings and knowing's will always align and agree with His word. The amount of time you choose to spend in His word and study it for yourself, will determine your growth in Christ and eventually greatly enhance your prayer life. I encourage you for when you pray, set your focus on Our Heavenly Father. Honor Him and Praise Him for His goodness and mercy. Bless Him for all that He has done for you and for all His gifts. Receive His word as your daily bread. As you enter worship, scripture says you are seated with Christ and are in the throne room of heaven. Allow time for Him to speak to you as well. This is why the reading of His word aloud is important in that the spoken word is powerful, it will come alive in you and will come back to you from the Father.

(W.E. Vine Expository Dictionary) - Prayer is properly addressed to God the Father Matt. 6:6; John 16:23; Eph. 1:17; 3:14, and the Son, Acts 7:59; 2 Cor. 12:8; but in no instance in the NT is prayer addressed to the Holy Spirit distinctively, for whereas the Father is in Heaven, Matt. 6:9, and the Son is at His right hand, Rom. 8:34, the Holy Spirit is in and with the believers, John 14:16,17... Prayer is to be offered in the Name of the Lord Jesus, John 14:13, that is, the prayer must accord with His character, and must be presented in the same spirit of dependence and submission that marked Him, Matt. 11:26; Luke 22:42... Faith is essential to prayer, Matt. 21:22; Mark 11:24; Jas. 1:5-8, for faith is the recognition of, and the committal of ourselves and our matters to, the faithfulness of God."

One example of praying the word of God for an acquaintance or loved one) –

"...Father in heaven, I give thanks for ____________, I desire to mention them in my prayer that you would give them the spirit of wisdom and revelation in the knowledge of our Lord Jesus Christ, the eyes of their understanding being enlightened, that they may know what is the hope of His calling, what are the riches of the glory of His inheritance in the saints, and what is the exceeding greatness of His power toward us who believe,..." Eph. 1: 17-19

And other great examples that can also be used as prayers are found in the book of Psalms, especially if you start with Psalms 23 and 91.

Chapter 5 – Acts ("Evangelism through the Holy Spirit")

Prior to preparing to write this chapter, I have had to take a step back and re-evaluate my past experiences related to the subject. The experiences were mostly based upon past negative influences while attending certain denominational churches and listening to their associated doctrines. It was not necessarily a matter of the other denomination's basic doctrine of Jesus and the cross. My experience and opinion are directed toward the peer pressure and the guilt-trip that is placed upon new converts to immediately go out after being saved.

At the time, as I recall, it was an attempt to follow their understanding of scripture in order to make other new converts. The basis of their doctrinal belief being that the exciting passionate testimony given by new converts would lead to more and create more new converts, thus adding to their numbers. Any attempts I made at the time were obviously unsuccessful. But the same could be said of the attempts made by others having similar results.

As a young teenager, one could say I was raised as a typical American teen. Once I accepted Jesus as my savior, I behaved and related more as a convert, in lieu of identifying as a disciple. As a teenager, I did have extremely low self-esteem from my upbringing at home. There was truly little available in the way of understanding how to receive follow up and to know how to grow in Christ. Admittedly, I became like my other friends and acquaintances, looking for acceptance and approval from those in my world. I was mainly interested in having fire insurance.

When I heard messages at church, I soon discovered later that there was a problem. The message preached really did not appear to be particularly good news. I did not really know much better but the messages given were manipulative, judgmental, and condemning. They had thoroughly convinced me I was an unworthy no-good sinner. With this, I honestly did not have much of a comprehension of what sin was, or what sins I had committed. I did not really know the Lord, or what really had happened to me at this conversion. I had an identity crisis as a young convert.

As a teenager, I was uncomfortable, without any confidence, nor any real knowledge in telling others, a depressing message of how bad and sinful they were and somehow that was going to convince them they needed a Savior. The junior and senior high school kids that I knew who had been converted during the mid to late 1970's, as time passed by, many of us grew lukewarm and cold by the time we had graduated. This experience is only part of the reason I had negative thoughts toward the ministry of evangelism.

We were taught the Great Commission. We heard it quite often. But, looking back at those messages, we honestly did not know what the Great Commission truly meant. If we would have read it for ourselves back then we might have clearly differentiated the meaning of the words convert and disciple. It is obvious they do not have the same meaning, yet they are used in Christian circles to have the same meaning.

There are several concepts and doctrines that have been used for the endeavor of church and personal evangelism, but in truth they are not. Many believers have been taught to impose upon those who do not believe. According to the Bible, evangelism is simply telling the good news of Christ. Coercion should not be the end goal but evangelism is only a proclamation and to be done in the love of God for lost souls. Believers are to present the gift of the gospel to all; we should not manipulate or force anyone to accept it. And we know we cannot coerce anyone into a life with Christ. Our job is to bring the message of Christ, it is the Holy Spirit who will work with us and move within the heart of people to hear and have faith for their salvation.

Another has been personal testimony, an extremely popular concept used to promote personal evangelism. This may contribute toward evangelism, but may also become a distraction from focusing on the facts and truth of the life, death, and resurrection of Christ. This usually ends up being more about the person and their life story than about Christ. Another has been the use of apologetics. Apologetics is giving answers to questions and defending objections about God or Christ. Apologetics is not evangelism. Political involvement and getting involved with social issues in this life are not evangelism. Becoming an activist for certain causes to save the lives of animals, or saving the planet are not evangelism.

Finally, the most common and dangerous mistake in evangelism is to misinterpret the results of evangelism for evangelism itself. That is the conversion of unbelievers. Making this error distorts well-meaning churches by turning them into results-oriented businesses. We must remember, it is all about Him.

Knowing that evangelism is part of all church ministry, there is a perspective I now lean toward and work from that are a basis for evangelism given from our Lord Jesus and the Apostle Paul. The following is one of several examples of what Paul considered the basis of "his gospel."

> Acts 17: 18-19 (NKJV), "Then, certain Epicurean and Stoic philosophers encountered him (Paul). And some said, "What does this babbler want to say?" Others said, "He seems to be a proclaimer of foreign gods," because he preached to them Jesus and the resurrection."

> Acts 17: 22-34 (NKJV), "Then Paul stood in the midst of the Areopagus and said, "Men of Athens, I perceive that in all things you are very religious; for as I was passing through and considering the objects of your worship, I even found an altar with this inscription: TO THE UNKNOWN GOD.

Therefore, the One whom you worship without knowing, Him I proclaim to you: "God, who made the world and everything in it, since He is Lord of heaven and earth, does not dwell in temples made with hands. Nor is He worshiped with men's hands, as though He needed anything, since He gives to all life, breath, and all things. And He has made from one blood every nation of men to dwell on all the face of the earth, and has determined their pre-appointed times and the boundaries of their dwellings, so that they should seek the Lord, in the hope that they might grope for Him and find Him, though He is not far from each one of us; for in Him we live and move and have our being, as also some of your own poets have said, 'For we are also His offspring.' Therefore, since we are the offspring of God, we ought not to think that the Divine Nature is like gold or silver or stone, something shaped by art and man's devising. Truly, these times of ignorance God overlooked, but now commands all men everywhere to repent, because He has appointed a day on which He will judge the world in righteousness by the Man whom He has ordained. He has given assurance of this to all by raising Him from the dead." And when they heard of the resurrection of the dead, some mocked, while others said, "We will hear you again on this matter." So Paul departed from among them. However, some men joined him and believed, among them Dionysius the Areopagite, a woman named Damaris, and others with them."

In this account, Holy Spirit reveals through Paul how evangelism should be introduced and how to talk to unbelievers about the gospel. In addition to this, Paul allows his evangelism to work in conjunction with being led by the Spirit in the message. The next scripture further reveals that the gospel was not presented in his own ability or his own wisdom, but in the power of the Spirit, as follows:

> 1Corinthians 2:1-5 (NKJV), "And I, brethren, when I came to you, did not come with excellence of speech or of wisdom declaring to you the testimony of God. For I determined not to know anything among you except Jesus Christ and Him crucified. I was with you in weakness, in fear, and in much trembling. And my speech and my preaching were not with persuasive words of human wisdom, but in demonstration of the Spirit and of power, that your faith should not be in the wisdom of men but in the power of God."

Finally, an explanation point to Paul's revelation is also found in Romans 1:16 identifying the gospel of Christ as the power of God to salvation for everyone who believes. I have come to believe in recent years, that there are whole denominations that have relied on their religious understanding, they have completely misunderstood and improperly communicated the message. They've improperly applied evangelism in the context of how the scriptures reveal this ministry. Evangelism is a stand-alone ministry gift and office as indicated in Ephesians. Jesus and Paul showed that evangelism works better as a complimentary work in unity with other ministry gifts. The message of evangelism should not be solely based upon the wisdom of men, or on our own understanding. The message should be communicated to build faith in the unbeliever that gives place for the power of God to rebirth the human spirit of the one hearing the message. (Romans 10).

Paul was gifted with the office of an evangelist along with the gifting of apostleship. At the same time, Paul encouraged believers that they should also follow in his manner of life, to imitate him as he imitated Christ. Jesus himself evangelized regularly. In Luke chapter 4, it reveals His custom was to enter the community synagogue and say, "The Spirit of the Lord is upon Me to preach the gospel to the poor; He has sent me to heal the brokenhearted, to proclaim liberty to the captives and recovery of sight to the blind, to set at liberty those who are oppressed; to proclaim the acceptable year of the Lord." At other times, He would preach and evangelize saying, "The time is fulfilled, and the kingdom of God is at hand. Repent, and believe in the Gospel." Then, He would proceed to heal the multitudes that received the message.

What point am I attempting to make? The point is that the Great Commission from our Lord was given to His disciples after His resurrection. This was after the disciples had been under the guidance and training of our Lord for over a three- and one-half-year period. This tells me new converts are needed, but they are not necessarily ready for evangelism. After the resurrection of Jesus, He still wanted the disciples to wait in Jerusalem until they had received the baptism of the Holy Spirit. They needed to be endued with the same power He had during His earthly ministry. This power would enable and empower them to "Go therefore and make disciples of all nations...." In my opinion, converts need time to learn and grow in Christ, becoming dedicated, empowered, and knowledgeable disciples of Christ, prior to embarking on any mission field.

There is another area of the ministry of evangelism that I believe tends to fall through the cracks in the local church. This is after the new convert has decided for the Lord, that is, the follow-up ministry of transition from new convert to discipleship. This is where the work begins, and it is also where they should be introduced to covenant relationship, communion and fellowship with their brothers and sisters in the Lord, assisting them with guidance and counsel, love and support, care, and teaching. Their relationship with the local church should and will mature and change just like their relationships with their spouse and or friends. Sometimes one thing will be needed; at another stage of life other kinds of support, correction, or instruction will be needed. Throughout it all, the new Christian should continue to be taught what it means to follow Jesus. From sitting under the preaching of the Word, to being baptized and taking the Lord's Supper, to praying and studying the Word, to repenting and believing. The good news is not merely about the beginning of an eternal relationship. Trusting Christ will always show itself by following Him throughout their lifetime.

The baptism, empowerment and the enablement of Holy Spirit should also be included within this process of follow-up and growth in Christ. In some Spirit-filled circles, there have been a few churches that have come to offer new believer classes, outreach classes and other Christian-growth classes that assist in building up new believers. But much more work needs to be done. Even the Apostle Paul admitted we are in need of many fathers in the faith.

Our culture today is much different than the ancient times of the early church. Reaching out to people is not as convenient as the city or town marketplaces of times past. Even though the so-called modern culture has become more connected via the internet and social media, I sense the culture has really become more isolated and introverted than ever before. I do not believe social media is the answer for evangelism. Just like in times past, today's culture not only needs personal evangelism on the local church level, but needs bold spirit-filled face to face encounters of evangelism that are necessary, in order for the Lord to work in the hearts of unbelievers on the city, county, state and national level as well.

There have been a few questions on my heart recently. Have there been any that are called to be evangelists that are trying to live their life as pastors and teachers? Has the prophetic movement become so large and overbearing where no one has time for evangelism? Where are the Spirit-filled and empowered evangelists of today? In the following scriptures, Paul wrote to the Thessalonians about how he and his associates had initially approached them with the gospel:

1 Thessalonians 1:5-9 (NKJV) "...For our gospel did not come to you in word only, but also in power, and in the Holy Spirit and in much assurance, as you know what kind of men we were among you for your sake. And you became followers of us and of the Lord, having received the word in much affliction, with joy of the Holy Spirit, so that you became examples to all in Macedonia and Achaia who believe. For from you the word of the Lord has sounded forth, not only in Macedonia and Achaia, but also in every place. Your faith toward God has gone out, so that we do not need to say anything. For they themselves declare concerning us what manner of entry we had to you, and how you turned to God from idols to serve the living and true God, ..."

Along with this scripture, there is another specific portion of scripture from the book of Acts in reference to Paul's first missionary trip and the encounter with the Thessalonians found in Acts chapter 17. The author Dr. Luke describes how Paul would "as his custom" first enter the local Synagogue of each community on the Sabbath to present evidence from the scriptures that Jesus was the Christ. Luke notes there were some Jews who were persuaded and others who were not. In addition, there were a multitude of devout Gentile Greeks that also followed and joined Paul. Then, as it happened elsewhere, the Jews who were not persuaded became envious and stirred up the evil men of the city and started a mob to seek out Paul and the others. The mob created an uproar and brought accusations claiming, (Acts 17:6) - "These men who have turned the world upside down have come here too." This was a serious charge, much closer to civil rebellion and it stirred up the local civil and the Roman authorities. This happened virtually everywhere Paul went in all of his journeys.

Even though we read about Paul reasoning and speaking with the Jews from the scripture in Acts, and though Luke does not mention this specifically, it is evident the Holy Spirit was fully at work through Paul in this endeavor. There are so many Christians in the body of Christ today, which have a problem with the previous statement. They tend to argue that the spoken word alone is powerful enough by itself to change lives. The spoken word of God is powerful, but the power that is backing up the word is the Spirit of God. They have a twisted understanding (2 Peter 3:16) in interpreting the scriptures, in that they deny the baptism and works of the Holy Spirit are for believers today. That the signs and wonders basically died with the apostles. Yet, out of the other side of their mouth they profess and passionately believe strongly in the indwelling of the Holy Spirit for salvation and the new birth.

If God's word is true for us today as it was back then, and says that God does not change, that Jesus is the same yesterday, today and forever, then the baptism, work and ministry of the Holy Spirit is the same today. He has never left His ministry in the earth since the day of Pentecost in Acts chapter 2. What has been the problem? Basically, the problem is with mankind and his dependence on his own intellect and the will of the flesh. In the church today, regarding evangelism, the approach has been out of alignment with the direction and instruction of the New Testament, especially with the examples given in Acts. Outreach and evangelism for the believer should be balanced based upon the ability "to rightly divide the word, to be led in the Spirit and walk in the power of the Spirit."

It does not matter how many doctorates and PhD's or letters there are after a person's name. Being trained in the scriptures and having the ability to reason and rightly divide the scriptures by human reasoning alone will not produce the same Holy Spirit results in a person's life as it is shown to us in Acts, which can be dangerous. According to Proverbs 3, relying on their own intellect, logic and understanding means they're not fully trusting the Lord with all their heart. This means their human reasoning will lead people into unbelief. This places many Christians in a hardship, because without faith, it is clear in Hebrews 11:6, that it is impossible to please God. The opposite of faith is unbelief and scripture warns us that if something is not of faith, it is sin. On the other hand, neither should someone be way out of balance in the opposite direction. These people attempt to "feel" the Spirit all the time. They're probably lacking a depth in understanding the word of God and in spiritual things. This is also incorrect and can be dangerous as well.

With regard to the importance of both the power of the Spirit and the truth of God's word working in each believer. This is to be provided for their preparation in the work of ministry and evangelism. A couple of examples are as follows with regard to their need for the baptism of the Holy Spirit. The first is given in the four gospel accounts of Matthew, Mark, Luke and John and the first few chapters of Acts by the example of the disciples themselves. They were around Jesus and participated in His ministry for three and one-half years, and still were unable to fully comprehend what was happening to them during the death, burial and resurrection of Jesus our Lord. In fact, Jesus had to return several more times after this to encourage and instruct them further on what was about to happen to them and the world. Before the day of Pentecost, they were men without the baptism of the Holy Spirit. They were men who probably had a basic to moderate understanding of or were familiar with the Pentateuch, the Law and the Prophets. They were not considered to be the theologians of their day. Jesus became their theologian. Israel was a theocracy, most children in Jewish society was instructed in the word of God. But, as we all know, the disciples scattered on the day Jesus allowed Judas and the mob to take Him away. They didn't understand, and neither would we if we had been there.

On the day of Pentecost, the disciples were assembled in one place, the Holy Spirit came on them with visible and audible signs. They spoke with new languages, so that their hearers were able to understand "the mighty works of God" (Acts 2:5-13). The coming of the Spirit was the fulfillment of the prediction of John (Luke 3:15-16) and the promise of Jesus (Luke 24:49). Peter declared it to be a fulfillment of the prophecy of Joel (Acts 2:16-21) and the proof of the resurrection of Christ (Acts 2: 32-36). They became emboldened to brave the perils of persecution (Acts 2:4; 4:8, 31; 6:8-15).

Not only were they emboldened, but they were also endued with power by the Spirit to walk their remaining life in the same manner as Jesus walked His life on earth. The other upper room believers were also included and baptized in the Holy Spirit. On that day, 3000 converts had been evangelized and became believers. They were added to their numbers and all believers in the early churches throughout the Roman Empire were baptized in the Holy Spirit. Subsequently after the day of Pentecost, other signs and wonders followed the apostles and believers, exactly as Jesus had promised beforehand.

Now, the second example of need for the baptism of the Holy Spirit comes from when Peter was called to go to the house of Cornelius, the Roman Centurion in Acts 10:17-48. In short, Cornelius was a devout Gentile man who honored God in his life, but now it was time for more and God had to shake Peter's foundation. This event opened Peter's mind to the fact that God desired evangelism and the power of the Holy Spirit to also extend to all men, both to the Jew and to the Gentile.

In summary of this chapter, the probable cause of success in the early church is identified as - the miraculous powers attributed to the early church. Signs and wonders from the Holy Spirit went hand in hand with the evangelism of new converts into the new faith. It wasn't just based upon the articulate spoken word of human reasoning and traditional religion. Conversion to the new faith came both by God's word and the ministry work (and power) of the Holy Spirit. The Book of Acts should be our model or example for understanding and practicing true evangelism. If you are new to this, I encourage you to be a disciple first, and allow yourself time to process and grow in the knowledge and wisdom of Christ. And allow yourself to experience the Baptism of the Holy Spirit that will bring your Counselor and Helper alongside you to empower and enable you in boldness and in speech. Let Him be your Guide in this rewarding endeavor. Be mindful of the fact that when you do pursue this evangelistic endeavor and ministry service, that there will be signs and wonders following you as mentioned in the Bible, because the Lord will be confirming His word through you with these signs following.

Here's another quote from John G. Lake that is fitting in closing this chapter – "The ministry [service] of the Christian [an anointed one] is the ministry of the Spirit [Holy Spirit]. He [the Christian] not only ministers words to another, but he ministers the Spirit of God. It is the Spirit of God that inhabits the words, which speaks to the spirit of another and reveals Christ in and through him."

Liardon, "John G. Lake," 227.

Conclusion –

Ephesians 4: 12, talks about "equipping saints" in the church. There is no reference to training "sinners" for the work of ministry. In Romans Chapter 1, Paul's letter to the church is addressed to those who are called "saints." The verses refer to believers in the church body as "saints." Yet, many in the body of Christ today still think of themselves as sinners first. Not many believe they are saints. Many people come from various doctrinal or denominational backgrounds that believe we are just sinners saved by grace based upon what that were taught or how they were raised from childhood. Many will believe that God can heal and some will say He does not heal today, others will only pray a wishful prayer - "if it be His will." Many think God uses sickness or disease to teach lessons to His people. It's simply not true. God has never stopped His healing ministry. The definition of "sinner" is simply one who misses the mark, or one who is walking this life in a lifestyle contrary to what God has established as His standard of living. Many believers live on a level of sin consciousness of not knowing who they are in Christ, not acquainted with the word of righteousness. That is, of being placed in a position of right-standing with God the Father through Christ. The word "saint" comes from the Greek word Hagioi, which simply means sanctified or holy one. Saint or sanctified one is a person who has been set apart from this world system and the devil's operation.

Again, allow a little clarification, all of us are on many different levels of faith, knowledge, and spiritual understanding. As long as we live in this flesh (our physical body), we are in a fight of faith and are to resist the devil and sin. After our new birth, as newborn babes, we did not know much of anything except maybe that Christ died for us. A growth process in Christ began from that moment onward. Can we all agree, that over the course of a lifetime, some will grow and mature in Christ, while others will choose to remain babes and only want what can be referred to as "fire insurance." As a saint, we should not deny we will have opportunities to sin, and are still capable of sinning, (1John 1: 8). But we have now been empowered by Holy Spirit to overcome sin and have been given the gift of repentance and forgiveness through our Advocate our Lord Jesus Christ. (1John 1: 8-10 and 1John 2: 5-6).

When an opportunity for evangelizing occurs be mindful of a few things regarding a couple religions and why people verbally curse –

Buddhism is based upon an endless upward systematic attempt to achieve or earn their salvation. It's basically a specialized complicated system of behavior modification. Recorded history indicates Buddha himself was originally a Hindu, but ran off and left his wife and child behind and eventually began this new so-called religion. The problem with Buddha, he is dead and is still in his grave.

Mohammad is credited with starting the Islamic religion via his personal demonic dreams, but even he had to have his dreams interpreted by others as to what they meant. He began as a peaceful religion at the first, imitating Christianity, but failed in convincing others. Later, he revised his religion to include threats of violence and murder of infidels who would not convert. He is revered as the main prophet, but also acknowledges Jesus Christ as a prophet as well. The problem with Mohammad, he is dead and is still in his grave.

Of all the various religions of the world, including Buddhism and Islam, Christianity is the only one that offers redemption via a Savior/ Messiah who died for our sins but was also raised from the dead, witnessed by 500 people after the resurrection and promised to return soon at the end of this age to gather his church for God's millennial kingdom on earth. This time period we're living in presently is referred to both the time of the Gentiles and the dispensation of God's grace. Jesus Christ is alive and will return.

Has anyone in this world or an unbeliever ever wondered why the name of 'Jesus Christ' is spoken or yelled aloud damning their circumstances in life? What people don't understand spiritually is the reason behind it. We hear perverse cursing almost on a daily basis. When they are spoken aloud, the enemy of our souls (the devil) receives that intended cursing as verbal praise for himself. He delights in the person who curses the Lord's Name. The effect of that cursing has on the heart of a person is it gradually dulls their heart and soul to the point of searing their conscience toward spiritual things. There comes a point where they simply reject any spiritual understanding. Nobody ever curses Buddha or Mohammad's name. It's always God- _____ this or that, or the name of Jesus is used. For us who believe, it's proof and a recognition of knowing that Jesus himself is alive. All other man-made religions of this world are dead.

A final word of encouragement, there is one verse of scripture that one should always keep in mind in their life, that is, "...if anyone thinks they're something, when they're really nothing, they're deceiving themselves." (Galatians 6:3 - NKJV) One might say this does not appear to be much of an encouragement, I would say hear what I am attempting to say for your own benefit and for good in the future. This verse goes against the grain of how people think and believe in our society today. Before anything else in our Christian walk, my encouragement to all would be to learn and develop an honest and true humility in Christ.

Humility is not self-abasement, or self-condemnation, and it does not come by osmosis nor are we born with it. Men and women are born into this world with pride in their nature. Some grow up into adulthood with their pride and arrogance a little more pronounced than others. Pride reveals itself in self-centeredness. Pride is all about an attitude of "me, I and my," it is based upon a self-centered life being all about the individual person. It is not necessarily recognizable to most people in this world and most of the time pride is subtle and not easily recognizable. Pride is what got Lucifer thrown out of heaven. Humility is all about being submitted to God and His word, being a willing servant of others, placing the needs of others first before our own, discovering and doing the will of God and discovering who we are in Christ. It is letting go and developing ourselves in Him. By developing humility and rejecting pride, in a lifestyle of repentance and of faith, a person can and will go far into the things and kingdom of God.

List of References from Public Domain and Copyright Materials

Text from the NKJV may be quoted in any form (written, visual, electronic, or audio) up to and inclusive of five hundred (500) verses or less without written permission, providing the text does not make up more than 25% of the total text in the work and the text is not being quoted in commentary or another Biblical reference work. This permission is contingent upon the appropriate copyright acknowledgement. www.harpercollinschristian.com[1]

No more than 500 verses quoted in total.

Scripture does not make up more than 25% of the total text.

Scripture does not account for an entire book of the Bible.

Scripture is not quoted in a commentary or any other Biblical Reference work.

All Scripture must be properly cited (see below).

Any use of the NKJV text must include a proper acknowledgement as follows:

Scripture taken from the New King James Version®. Copyright © 1982 by Thomas Nelson. Used by permission of HarperCollins Christian Publishing.

All rights reserved.

The text of the Amplified Bible may be quoted in any form (written, visual, electronic or audio) up to and inclusive of five hundred (500) verses without express written permission of the publisher, providing the verses do not amount to a complete book of the Bible nor do the verses quoted account for more than 25% of the total work in which they are quoted. Scripture notations taken from the Amplified* Bible, Classic Edition*

---

1. *http://www.harpercollinschristian.com*

---

2. *http://www.Lockman.org*

3. *http://www.harpercollinschristian.com/*

---

4.   http://www.whitakerhouse.com/

5.   http://www.whitakerhouse.com/

About the Author

A church layman with experience of over 50 years in various denominational and non-denominational churches. Later in his life, God called Mark to attend Covenant University based in Hudson, Florida, formerly known as Covenant Bible College and Seminary. Mark successfully achieved both a Bachelor of Science and a Master of Art's, each in Biblical Theology. The university is operated in association with Jonathan Vorce Ministries.